BOYS
of the
BRIGADE
VOLUME ONE

A Portrait in Old Photographs & Picture Postcards

Robin Bolton

S.B. Publications

The Boys' Brigade

Remember now thy CREATOR

In the days of thy YOUTH.

SURE & STEDFAST

1st Aberfeldy.
Company

Session 1903-4

PRIZE

For *Good attendance*

AWARDED TO

Private John Keir

Captain

Cover Picture: 68th London Coy. B.B. c1925.
Frontispiece: A Private of Grimsby St. John's C.L.B.

This book is dedicated to my Father.
and
Those thousands of Brigade Officers and Voluntary Youth Workers who have dedicated much of their 'spare' time and energy for the benefit of our young people.

First published in 1991by S.B. Publications
Unit 2, The Old Station Yard,
Pipe Gate,
Market Drayton,
Shropshire, TF9 4HY

British Library Cataloguing in Publication Data
Boys of the Brigade.
1. Great Britain. Christianity. Organisations. History
I. Bolton, Robin
267. 70941

ISBN 1-870708-50-4

Printed and bound by Warwick Printing Co. Ltd., Theatre Street, Warwick.

BOYS of the BRIGADE

VOLUME ONE

Contents

Back Cover Picture: Good times at a Bolton B.B. Camp 1930's [Dave Thomas]

Acknowledgements

This book would not have been produced without the help of the individuals and organizations listed below. I would also like to thank the many Brigade, Battalion and Company Secretaries etc, Serving Officers, Old Boys and relatives of Old Boys who have so willingly contributed information and literature, accompanied by countless wonderful stories.

THE BOYS' BRIGADE

Rev. Bob Allaway, Llanbradach.
John Cooper, Glasgow Battalion B.B. Archivist
Alan D. Hambly, Cardiff.
Stephen Hulcoop, Harlow, Essex.
Herbert Ingham. Halifax.
Stephen Lane, Boys' Brigade Archivist. Barnet.
R.K. Lolley, Leeds
Len Lyndsey, Edinburgh
London District B.B. Office Kennington.
George Oakton, Birmingham
E. Roose, Liverpool B.B.
Barry St-John-Nevill. B.B. H.Q.
Charles Williamson. Bridge of Weir.

THE CHURCH LADS' BRIGADE & LONDON DIOCESAN CHURCH LADS' BRIGADE

David Blake, Bebington, Wirral.
Alan Bull, Edmonton, London.
Neville Gray, Lincoln.
David Harris. C.L.B. H.Q.
Manchester Public Library
Warrington Public Library
Les Worthington. Gorton, Manchester.

THE JEWISH LADS' BRIGADE

K. Drapkin, Birmingham.
Mrs. T. Galena, Birmingham.
Mrs. R. Kaplan, Birmingham.
Mike Kaplan, Birmingham.
Mike Lamm, Provincial Adjutant, Birmingham.
Martin Robins, Archivist. J.L.B. H.Q. London.
Richard Weber, J.L.B. H.Q. London.

THE CATHOLIC BOYS' BRIGADE

Fr. David Lannon. Salford Diocesan Archivist
Fr. Michael Clifton. Southwark Archdiocesan Archivist.

THE BOYS' LIFE BRIGADE

Keith Walcott, Tooting.
Rev. B. Ranford, Tooting.

THE BOYS' OWN BRIGADE

David Ballantyne, Christchurch.
Dr. Rollo Ballantyne. Chipping Camden.
Rev. Andrew Hill, Edinburgh, Unitarian Historical Society.

ACKNOWLEDGEMENTS – CONTINUED

Liverpool Library & Record Office
A.S. Moore, Liverpool.
Alan Ruston, Watford.
F.M. Ryde Vanburgh Park, London
E. Basil Short, Chepstow.
Rev. Francis Simons. Essex Church, Kensington
Trevor Watkins, Sompting.
Raymond Williams, Southall, London
Trustees, Dr Williams' Library, London.

THE BOLSOVER COLLIERY CO. BOYS' BRIGADE

Ken Davies, Rainworth, Notts.
Paul Galant, Rainworth, Notts.
Mansfield Public Library, Local Studies Dept.

THE YOUNG LIFE PIONEERS & THE LIFE SAVING BRIGADE

Reg Feasey, Romford.
Arthur Casson.
Alice Duxbury, Batley.

THE BOLTON BOYS' BRIGADE

Ronnie, Halliwell, Bolton, B.B.
Dave Thomas, Bolton.
Harry Yates, Westhoughton.

THE NEW CHURCH BOYS' BRIGADE

Neville Gray, Lincoln.
Rev Bruce Jarvis, Sunderland.
Gordon Jacobs, Birmingham.
Gordon Kuphal Archivist, Swedenborg Soc/New Church, London.
Howard W. Turner

THE CHORLEY BRIGADES

Jack Beasley, Chorley.
Rev. James Burns, St Peter's Chorley.
Chorley Public Library
Philip J. Dickinson. St. Peter's C.L.B.

GENERAL/MILITARY ETC. & C.L.B.

Mike Wells, Ashby-de-la-Zouch.

MARKETING, GENERAL ADVICE ETC.

Steve Benz, S.B. Publications

Photographs etc.

The photographs, picture postcards and ephemera used in this book are taken from the author's own collection except where indicated in brackets under each item. The author is indebted to these various organizations and individuals who have kindly loaned or donated material.

THE AUTHOR: Robin G.A. Bolton

Born in Walsall in 1949 Robin joined the 57th Birmingham (Pheasey) Coy The Boys Brigade as a 'Life Boy' in 1957, serving through the ranks to become a Lieutenant. The 57th B'ham Coy. in the 1970's was one of Britain's largest, most successful and progressive BB Coys; providing Robin with a unique opportunity to participate in the leadership of a whole range of Brigade activities. In 1976 he founded the Brigade's National Band Contest as one result of developing and teaching the Company Band.

As an active leader in and writer about, the Youth Band movement, Robin was for some years a council member of the British Youth Band Association for some of the time Vice-Chairman. In the 1980's he helped to administer, promote and teach the avant-garde American Style 'Drum & Bugle Corps' activity through the auspices of the 'Drum Corps United Kingdom' organization and as Corps Director of the 'Cavaliers' Drum Corps and later as Corps Manager of 'The Beechmen' Drum Corps. For two years Robin served as The U.K.'s European Drum Corps Representative, helping to form the 'Drum Corps Deutschland' organization in Germany.

Recently, Robin has moved out of the Drum Corps activity. Time formerly spent organising contests and tours has now been re-directed. A new venture in 'Community Circus' for young people employs his skills in instruction ... from brass instruments to stilt-walking. As circus manager he can be found negotiating times for fire-jugglers to perform at a festival in Kent one weekend whilst helping to cook meals for 40 in a field in Lancashire the next!

Robin graduated from Birmingham University in 1971 after studying Geography, Art & Education at St Peter's College. He is currently teaching at Dartmouth High School, Great Barr, a Comprehensive School with more than 1700 pupils.

An avid writer and researcher of both local and Boys' Brigade history Robin started acquiring Brigade Picture Postcards about fifteen years ago and has built up an extensive collection.

Introduction

In our late twentieth century High Streets and old innercity areas stand the hardly-used and the abandoned Victorian Churches and Chapels. Majestic in their decorated brick and stone; mausoleums to those revivalist congregations of respectable clerks, artisans and their progeny who filled them to capacity on the Lord's Day, splendidly arrayed in their 'Sunday Best'. It was these folks, 'working for the Lord' in their magnificent edifices, who in order to perpetuate their own pious values, nurtured the Boys' Brigades.

This is the first volume of a two volume set. I started out originally to write a single volume, but such was the wealth of information, it has of necessity been bisected. This work concentrates on the various 'Brigades', their growth and organization, interesting in itself, but supplying the essential contextual background to the 'activities' featured in volume two.

Picture postcards make up a large part of the photographic record in these volumes. The 'Golden-Age' of the Picture Postcard corresponds almost exactly with the start of the great re-discovery and re-definition of Boyhood and Adolescence that we now take for granted. Consequently, there is a profusion of pictures of young people engaged in specifically 'youth' activities. I have focused upon the 'Brigade Movement' which was an important influence on many thousands of Boys.

In the closing decade of the nineteenth and the first twenty years of the twentieth century hopes were high in the Church and perhaps Government, that the 'new invention' of the uniformed youth organizations led by Smith's Boys' Brigade would be the avant-garde of the new working class generation, set to save the crumbling British Empire.

Expectations for the nation's exploding boy population were high, despite the fact that the majority lived in mighty industrial cities; sprawling soot-caked conurbations eating into the countryside. Urban living, it had been said, resulted in youths with 'sunken chests' and such decline in the nation's youth would lead directly to decline in the Empire.

The new Brigades were seen to epitomise all the traditional values in late Victorian society. They would, it was stated, cement national unity and reinforce social conformity amongst the working classes... this is at a time when Socialism at home looked more dangerous than the German Empire did abroad.

There were those who did not approve, however, they didn't stop to examine the advantages of the Brigades; they worried and complained about the growth of Christian Militarism, 'serving both God and the devil' However, the Brigades caught on, in a big way. Perhaps they had the better advocates. This defence of the Boys Brigade appeared in 1899:

'Contrary to a somewhat national impression, the Boys' Brigade does not teach the "Art of War" nor does it foster or encourage the war spirit. It simply employs military organisation, drill and discipline as the most stimulating and interesting means of securing the attention of a volatile class, and of promoting self-respect, chivalry, courtesy, esprit-de-corps and a host of kindred virtues... Firemen are drilled, Policemen are drilled, and though it is true the cap and belt of the boys are the regalia of another order, it may be doubted whether drill is any more to them than to these other sons of peace.'

War-like spirits may not have existed amongst the boys, but in the country as a whole the military were generally held in awe. G.A. Henty, the doyen of the robust boys adventure at the time, held up those ideals of manliness and courage which appealed to a young populous weaned on the heroic and romantic exploits of General Gordon and the like. Books and magazines of the period were laden with the 'glamour' associated with pre 1914 warfare. Lt Gen. Baden-Powell, national hero of the siege of Mafeking was quick to associate himself with the Brigades. (Both Henty & Baden-Powell were Boys Brigade Vice-Presidents). The motto of the whole generation seems to have been (like the Boys' Own Brigade): 'Quit you like men; be strong!'

Perhaps the most important and inescapable fact was that lads were attracted to the Brigades (Some 120,000 plus by 1914) they enjoyed what they were doing. At a time before the age of universal entertainment, post thirteen education, cheap transport or holidays, the Brigades provided an extra dimension to the mundane routine of the factory, shop & office or boredom of the street. The natural sense of belonging to a gang was an instinct exploited to great effect by the Brigades using the interest-grabbing pursuits of Physical Drills, Music, Football, Clubroom, Ambulance, Pioneering and the highlight of the year, the Annual Summer Camp.

Boys could really be 'somebody' as a member of a Brigade Company. To many employers Brigade Boys were 'model' employees, good citizens... public school virtues alive and well in the working class! Brigade membership could well be seen as a meal-ticket for the future.

The Boys' Brigade launched the 'Brigade Movement' in Britain, and there were a number of outwardly similar clones which grew up before the turn of the century. Activities, aims and leadership varied considerably; perhaps most markedly in their attitude to increasing militarism as the country drifted inevitably towards the Great War. Offshoots and short-lived localised variants were very common. Notably the growth of 'Scouting' as an activity found its roots in the Brigades, where it continued to grow even after 'B.P.'s Scouts' formed their own Patrols after 1907.

I have endeavoured to satisfy a number of conflicting aims and interests within the limitation of these volumes; a wide spread of organizations, activities, dates and locations. Many pictures chose themselves by virtue of their outstanding quality and captivating interest. I make no apologies for including these, perhaps at the expense of some of my other aims.

There already exists much first-class published material covering the development of The Boys' Brigade; the result of research undertaken for the Centenary in 1983, albeit short on photographic illustration. I have chosen, therefore, to illuminate, often with unique photographic evidence, some of the Brigades hitherto somewhat marginalised or totally ignored.

By 1950 the age of the 'Brigade' picture-postcard was over; the same increasing affluence which was to transform youthwork and youth culture swept aside the need for postcards as a means of essential communication, threatening the very raison d'etre of the Brigades themselves.

Just as some Churches and Chapels endured, surviving the "Change and decay ... all ... around ..." 'particularly the redevelopment of the 1960's; so too some of the Brigades survive', their companies marching into an age when piety, conformity and loyalty are all being debased and the habits of Reverence, Obedience and Discipline rarely associated with young people.

R.G.A. Bolton.
Little Aston,
South Staffordshire.

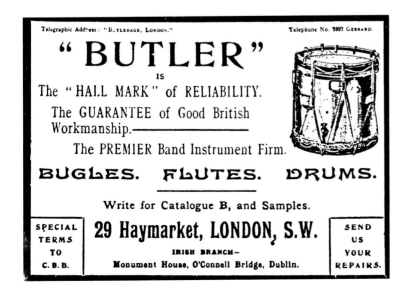

The Founder of The Boys' Brigade

Sir William A. Smith.

"You have only one life to live on earth, therefore be determined by God's help to make your life a success."

SIR WILLIAM ALEXANDER SMITH 1854 – 1914

Father of the Brigade Movement

There would, probably have been no Boys' Brigade or even Boy Scouts for that matter, had it not been for the foresight of the 'Pioneer of Boyhood' & Father of the Brigade Movement, William Alexander Smith.

Born in a remote Scottish farmhouse, only hours after the fateful Bugle call had signalled Lord Cardigan's famous charge of the Light Brigade; Smith's background had all the trappings of militarism. His father was a member of the 'Volunteers and young William was destined to follow his father's footsteps. At the age of nineteen, when working in his uncle's business in Glasgow, he was appointed Lance Corporal in the 1st Lanarkshire Rifle Volunteers. That same year saw him 'Join the Church' a result of a visit to hear evangelists Moody & Sankey.

By 1883 William had become 'Lt Smith' and was also teaching at the North Woodside Mission Sunday School, where his friends described him as a man of 'exceptional personality'. The Boys in his Sunday School Class were something of a challenge however, they 'declined to be controlled' and had not even a 'nodding acquaintance' with discipline. Bill Smith was open to suggestions. 'Perhaps… said a friend, 'the methods you use in the Volunteers could be employed in the Sunday School?' 'Why should it be easy for a man to control a hundred other men on a Saturday afternoon and so difficult to control a mere handful of Boys on the Sunday!'

Smith had found his answer… and his calling. 'Esprit-de-Corps', discipline. Here was a military model which could be used effectively with the twelve-seventeen year old working class Boy that would produce all the same 'virtues' as did Dr Arnold in his Rugby school.

Smith's 'new invention' The Boys' Brigade was formed on the 4th October 1883. Boys were soon to flock to this and other Brigades modelled on it, in their thousands.

In 1909 he was knighted by King Edward VII for his services to Boys. Sir William died suddenly after being taken ill at a Brigade meeting in London.

First photograph of The Boys' Brigade – 1st Glasgow Company at Garscube House, 9th April 1885.

[Reproduced with the kind permission of the Brigade Secretary of The Boys' Brigade]

Annals of the Brigade Movement 1860-1990

Date	Notes
1860	William Quarrier, WORKING BOYS' BRIGADE (Uniformed) Glasgow, Baptist.
1861	GLASGOW FOUNDRY BOYS Meetings (Non Uniformed) Mary Ann Clough
1862	
1863 }	Various BRIGADES formed. SHOE BLACK B. PARCELS B. NEWS B. Also COTTAGE HOMES
1864 }	(For orphans) started. Military style uniform
1865	GLASGOW FOUNDRY BOYS RELIGIOUS. SOCIETY. Cap, Belt, Haversack uniform introduced.
1866	
1867	
1868	
1869	
1870	FOUNDRY BOYS Uniform disappears. Org. continues to flourish.
1871	FOUNDRY BOYS called WORKING BOYS & GIRLS RELIGIOUS SOCIETY .
1872	
1873	
1874	
1875	
1876	
1877	
1878	
1879	
1880	
1881	
1882	
1883	4th Oct. THE BOYS' BRIGADE founded. 1st Glasgow Coy. William A Smith. 13-17 yr olds.
1884	Some Junior Orgs. of BB are formed (Unofficial) Some (Unofficial) BB Cadets too. First BB Uniform Introduced.
1885	First BB Band. G.A Henty. BB Vice-President. GORDON BB Started in Liverpool.
1886	Peak year for FOUNDRY BOYS (16,000 Boys & Girls) EAST LONDON CADET CORPS founded.
1887	BB Started in USA (Later to become 'United Boys' Brigades of America')
1888	
1889	THE GORDON BOYS BRIGADE founded in Southampton by Sir Charles Wilson KCB. Also in Portsmouth.
1890	SOUTHWARK CADETS founded at the Red Cross Hall by Octavia Hill & others.
1891	11th November CHURCH LADS' BRIGADE Formed in Fulham by Walter Mallock Gee. (C. of E. Temperance) LONDON DIOCESAN CHURCH LADS' BRIGADE Formed, by Col. Everard Ford. Liverpool GORDON BB merged into CLB. 1ST LONDON CADET BATTALION formed. (Merger of E. London & Southwark).
1892	THE GIRLS' BRIGADE formed (In Dublin – Ireland only!)
1893	
1894	BB Had 30,000 members.
1895	JEWISH LADS' BRIGADE formed. East London, Col Albert Edward Goldsmid (In Conjunction with the Maccabean Soc)
1896	CATHOLIC BOYS' BRIGADE formed. Sept. Bermondsey, Rev Father Felix Segesser. NEW CHURCH BOYS BRIGADE formed. 'A' Coy. Rev. G.B. Meek B.A., Kearsley, N. Manchester. Approx Start of BOLSOVER COLLIERY CO. BOYS' BRIGADE, Nottinghamshire.
1897	BOYS LIFE GUARDS formed. Colne, Lancs. Rev. T.A. Leonard. ('Father of the Open Air Movement')
1898	J.L.B. Expands, New Provincial Units formed.
1899	Lord Meath's LADS' DRILL ASSOCIATION formed. JLB Spreads outside London. October, BOYS' OWN BRIGADE Formed. (Unitarian) Lambeth. Rev. J.C. Ballantyne. BOYS' LIFE BRIGADE Formed. Rev John Brown Paton. Nottingham, formed under auspices of National Sunday School Union.
1900	GIRLS' GUILDRY Founded, Dr William Francis Somerville. (With Boys' Brigade)
1901	BOYS NAVAL BRIGADE & LONDON NEWSBOYS BRIGADE (Formed 1901-1906) C.N.A.B. THE CHURCH NURSING AND AMBULANCE BRIGADE FOR YOUNG WOMEN & GIRLS, Formed. Kilburn. Rev. Thomas Milner.
1902	GIRLS' LIFE BRIGADE formed. (In England) Baden-Powell Appointed BB Vice President. B.L.B. CADETS introduced. (10-12 yr. olds)
1903	BOYS RIFLE BRIGADE Leeds. Gordon Boys Build H.Q. in Southsea. B.P. Attends BB London Display at Royal Albert Hall. October. GIRLS' AUXILIARY BRIGADE (New Church) Formed. No. 1 Coy at Salford, Lancs.
1904	BB Strength 55,000.
1905	
1906	'SCOUTING FOR BOYS' Appears in B.B. Gazette. CLB Membership 45,000.

1906	LONDON DIOCESAN CLB Membership 7,000
	BOYS BRIGADE SCOUT PATROLS formed (Within existing BB Coys).
1907	SCOUTING FOR BOYS published for use with Brigades & YMCA etc. B.P. SCOUTS Started informally, Brownsea Island 'Scout' Camp. (Run by Baden-Powell)
	More than 4,000 BB Boys & 400 Officers were involved in 'Scouting'
1908	Catholic BB Strength estimated at 8,000. (Half in Ireland)
	IMPERIAL LADS BRIGADE West Hartlepool.
	CLB Reached peak strength of 70,000 in 1,300 Companies.
	BOLTON BB Withdrew from BB, became independent.
	THE SCOUT ASSOCIATION Started.
1909	Attempts start to incorporate BB into Govt. CADET SCHEME
	BB Scouting Uniform Officially approved.
	CLB started 'INCORPORATED CHURCH SCOUT PATROLS'
1910	Scouts membership now 108,000, GIRL GUIDES formed.
	Sir Francis Vane's 'NATIONAL PEACE SCOUTS' (British Boy Scouts & BLB Scouts) formed.
1911	CLB Affiliated to Govt. TERRITORIAL CADET SCHEME. 36,000 members.
	L.D.C.L.B. Enter Cadet Scheme as the CHURCH CADET BRIGADE.
1912	B.L.B. SCOUTS Recognised as a corporate body within the Boys Life Brigade. (Due to failure of National Peace Scouts).
1913	BOYS' OWN BRIGADE JUNIOR CORPS founded, Liverpool. Hill St Mission
	CLB Khaki Dress Uniform Adopted.
	CLB JUNIOR TRAINING CORPS started.
	GIRLS' OWN BRIGADE Formed. New Gravel Pit Unitarian Church. Hackney. Miss E.H. Green.
1914	BB Has 868 Bands and membership of 66,000
	I.C.S.P. Taken back into CLB as part of organisation. (Dress & Training retained)
	BLB Membership 15,000, Scouts 160,000
	JLB Affiliates to Army Cadets (Royal Fusiliers & Provincial Regiments.)
	LIFE-SAVING SCOUTS formed, Col. Sladen. (Salvation Army)
	Battalion of KING'S ROYAL RIFLE CORPS Recruited from C.L.B. members & ex-members.
1915	Junior Orgs. of BB (Still Unofficial) are popular. (Called 'Cadet Corps') BROWNIES Formed. (With Girl Guides) First CLB Naval Company formed, Folkestone, including a training Corps. Rev. C.J. Offer & Lt. D.A.H. Lawrance.
1916	WOLF CUBS Recognised as Official by the Scout Association.
	BRITISH BOY SCOUTS (Pacifist) Formed.
	WOODCRAFT GROUPS (Pacifist) founded by Ex Boy Scout Leaders.
1917	BB CADET COYS approved. Khaki Uniform. (BB Coys had free choice about affiliating to Govt Cadets)
	BOY RESERVES formed (Junior Reserve of BB) by Carey Longmore. (9-12 yr olds) Composed of 'Sections'.
	LONDON DIOCESAN CLB became 'Associated' with CLB.
1918	CLB almost 'Wiped out' by war-service.
1919	LONDON DIOCESAN CLB Amalgamated with CLB. BB Regulation Grey (Alternative) Uniform adopted B.P. ROVER SCOUTS started. Scouts increasing numerically.
1920	LIFEBOYS Founded. (Junior Org of BLB) Composed of 'Teams' divided into groups.
	BROTHERHOOD OF BRITISH BOY SCOUTS. Founded P.H. Pooley. (Sabbatarian)
1921	CADET CORPS re-vitalised. Govt. Grants start to be withdrawn from Brigades etc.
1922	
1923	Cadet Grant withdrawn from CLB.
	C.N.A.B. re-formed into CHURCH GIRLS' BRIGADE.
1924	Blue Uniform Introduced in CLB Co-op movement Catford. BB membership 77,000, Scouts 282,000.
	Cadet Coys of BB Discontinued.
	St. Peter's & St Lawrence (Chorley) C.L.B. Join National Organization.
1925	3rd Feb. WOODCRAFT FOLK started. Pacifist, anti-militarist, anti BP. Inf. from Ernest Thompson Seton (Socialist org.) CLB down to 18,000.
	Boys Own Brigade, Absorbed into Boys' Clubs etc.
1926	'Dummy' (Model) Rifles discontinued in BB. By 31st May.
	BB & BLB Amalgamate (1st Oct.). BB 90,000 BLB 29,000. Juniors called LIFE BOYS.
	BB.'A'. & 'B' Uniforms Adopted (Discontinued: 1941 [Life Boys] 1968 [Other Sections])
1927	Catholic BB being absorbed into Catholic Scouts & Boys Guilds at end of Territorial Cadet Scheme.
	BB Scouting Uniform discontinued.
	YOUNG LIFE PIONEERS Formed (Ex. BLB). Mainly N. London. Affiliated to British Boy & Girl Scouts. Other 'LIFE SAVING BRIGADES' formed.
1928	St. James C.L.B. (Chorley) joins national C.L.B.
1929	
1930	Youth Hostels started to grow rapidly.
	BRITISH NATIONAL CADET ASSOCIATION founded. CLB Cadet recognition withdrawn.
	CLB Cadet Recognition restored by (optional) affiliation to BNCA.
	Life Saving Scouts 2nd largest woodcraft movement.
1931	
1932	BB 'Regulation Grey' Uniform Discontinued 31st Dec.

1933	Scouts reach Peak numbers, 461,000 in U.K.
1934	Boys' Brigade reach Peak numbers, 163,000 in U.K.
1935	New Blue Uniform adopted as standard for all CLB. Companies (Except N. Ireland)
1936	CLB's Affiliation to Army Cadets ceases. (Khaki uniform finished).
	CLB. YOUNG BOYS' CORPS started.
	CLB Re-Constituted.
1937	Govt. Grants to Youth Organizations re-established.
1938	Young Life Pioneers (Mainly Bands) re-united with BB or Peace Scouts
1939	BOLSOVER COLLIERY CO. B.B. Suspended.
1940	
1941	AIR SCOUTS formed. Wartime compulsory registration in Youth Orgs. Gordon BB Ceased in Portsmouth.
1942	
1943	
1944	
1945	ARMY CADET FORCE Formed. Sponsored by Army, affiliated to Territorials.
1946	
1947	BOLSOVER COLLIERY CO. B.B. Finished. (Nationalization of Coal Mines).
1948	LIFE SAVING SCOUTS & GUIDES Incorporated into mainstream Scouting as S.A. Scouts.
1949	
1950	
1951	
1952	
1953	
1954	
1955	CLB in rapid decline during all 1950's.
1956	
1957	
1958	
1959	Last recorded CBB Unit in U.K. (Band. St. Mary's Failsworth, Nr Oldham Lancs.)
1960	Albermarle Report on YOUTH SERVICE ('Large Youth Orgs & Youthwork 'lack imagination')
	BOLTON BB Re-Joins The Boys' Brigade.
1961	CBB Assumed to be absorbed into Scouts, Youth Clubs etc. Except for SALESIAN BB (Malta)
1962	
1963	JEWISH GIRLS BRIGADE Formed. Newsom Report Published.
1964	BB Haynes Report (Future of BB) Published.
1965	Unity of Girls' Brigade, Girls' Guildry, & Girls' Life Brigade. GIRLS' BRIGADE formed.
	Life Boys minimum age reduced to 8 yrs.
1966	Sept. 1st/17th. Life Boys disappear to become JUNIOR SECTION BB. COMPANY SECTION & SENIOR SECTION Formed.
	Scouts Advance Party Report. (New Uniforms,) Boy Scouts become SCOUTS, Wolf Cubs become CUB SCOUTS, Senior Scouts become VENTURE SCOUTS.
	CLB Bishop of Exeter's Committee on present day appeal. Report published.
1967	
1968	New-style Awards introduced in the BB.
1969	
1970	BP SCOUTS Formed. (Breakaway, group opposed to 'modern scouting').
	BB New Uniform Hats Introduced. Standard for all three sections. (Junior, Company, Senior)
1971	
1972	
1973	
1974	JEWISH LADS' & GIRLS BRIGADE Formed. (Amalgamation).
1975	
1976	
1977	Pre-Junior Organisations of BB Accepted & recognised. (Various names, 'Robins, Cabin Boys' etc)
1978	Church Lads' Brigade & Church Girls' Brigade wound up. New organisation formed:
	CHURCH LADS' & CHURCH GIRLS' BRIGADE. (November)
1979	
1980	
1981	
1982	Pre-Junior BB (6-8 yrs). Officially Called ANCHOR BOYS. 1st Oct. Scouts form BEAVERS for 6-8 yr olds (In 'Colonies')
1983	New Awards Introduced into BB Company Section.
1984	
1985	
1986	
1987	
1988	
1989	
1990	Scout Association allow girls to join. (Previously only allowed in 'Venture' Section).
1991	Boys' Brigade consider continuation of allowing Girls to participate in activities.

1. THE BIG BRIGADES

Boys' Brigade Inspection at Glasgow, 27th April, 1912.

LORD INVERCLYDE.

EARL SHAFTESBURY.

SIR WILLIAM SMITH.
(FOUNDER OF BOY'S BRIGADE)

THE BOYS' BRIGADE

1883-1926

1926 –

Object: *'The advancement of Christ's Kingdom among Boys and the promotion of habits of Obedience, Reverence, Discipline, Self-Respect and all that tends towards a true Christian Manliness.'*

Motto: 'Sure & Stedfast'

The Boys' Brigade was founded on 4th October 1883 at the North Woodside Mission Hall in Glasgow by William Alexander Smith. It was originally intended to be for the Boys attending that mission alone, to solve a problem faced by Smith in trying to cope with teaching teenage Boys in his Sunday school class. Fifty-nine Boys joined in the first few weeks with thirty five staying on and agreeing to firm regulations. There was no distinctive uniform in the first year.

To say that it was successful would be an under statement! Other Churches in Glasgow and throughout Scotland quickly took up the idea. By 1885 Companies in England were formed, the first in London. After five years 206 Coys existed. In 1887 the B.B. had established itself in Wales, at Newport, by 1888 the 1st Belfast had been formed closely followed in 1889 by 1st Dublin. After ten years the membership stood at a massive 26,000 Boys. By 1934 it was 96,762 and 1944 77,998 (11-18 yr olds.)

The Anchor Crest, & motto were taken from the Authorised version of the Epistle to the Hebrews, Chapter 6 v 19. The Red Cross of the Boys' Life Brigade was added in 1926, the only change in over one hundred years.

From the outset the B.B. has been a Church based organization, interdenominational among the Protestant Churches. Substantial support was received in the early years from many areas of Public Life. Patronage from King George V and the Archbishop of Canterbury.

B.B. Boy 1886.
Officer 1893.

[The Boys' Brigade Glasgow Battalion]

Boys from the 9th 32nd Glasgow Coys. The Boys' Brigade c1890
[The Boys' Brigade, Glasgow Battalion]

Members of the 32nd Glasgow Coy. B.B. c1890
[The Boys' Brigade, Glasgow Battalion]

SIGNING ON...

'Signing on'

A coloured postcard produced by Valentines of Dundee, one of a set illustrating Boys Brigade activities in the early 1900's. Subjects include 'Marching Orders', 'Rifle Drill', 'On Guard', 'A Raid on the Canteen' & 'Off Duty'. The posed scenes were taken in or near Baxter Park, Dundee, all with one of the Boys seen wearing the kilt.

Signing On

The start of a Boy's life in the 'Brigade'. When you enrolled in a Boys' Brigade Company you were signing up to become part of a large family. Life now had another dimension. This family was a 'Company' of perhaps a hundred members aged from thirteen or fourteen to nineteen. A Boy joined as a 'recruit' and gradually progressed to full membership as 'Private' along with which came the responsibilities of attendance, observing the Object, Company rules, etc and of course, the exciting advantages of a Uniform or 'equipment' as it was often known and the manifold activities for which you were immediately entitled.

A 'Company' was the basic working unit of all the 'Brigades'. It was often broken down into squads or grouped with others into Battalions and Districts. Local loyalty and specific activities could thus thrive within this framework whilst outwardly displaying a common format.

Contrary to some widely held opinions, most Boys were recruited from the families of reasonably well to do 'artisans' and not from the Street Urchins of Glasgow and other major cities. It was only this relative wealth which made it possible for Boys to occupy their 'leisure time' in a Brigade Company.

Parents were not, however, wealthy enough to purchase a 'full military uniform' for their Boy, nor was it considered desirable. The BB Uniform set the standard for 'Brigades' all over the Nation with its 'Equipment' of Black Forage (Pill Box) hat with two white rings of braid. White canvas Haversack, & Brown Leather Belt modelled on the uniform of the local 'Volunteers'. Worn over the 'normal clothing' (usually 'Sunday best') it was thought to present clearly to its critics a picture that was not overtly 'military' in nature; but simply using military ideas as a 'means to an end' and thus reflecting the spirit of the Brigade.

Two young B.B. Privates. c1908

4th Brighton (Hove) Coy. 1910-1911.

This postcard produced by E. Pannell of Hove shows a successful Company with their trophies and equipment. The stretcher has the Coy. details along with its own name: 'The Grace' presented by Nurse Spurgeon 1910. Note the carbines, bar-bells, dumb-bells, and the little mascot dog equipped with his own pill box!

An original Membership Application Form. 1883...

All members 'carried the card'

THE BOYS' BRIGADE.

FORM OF APPLICATION FOR MEMBERSHIP.

I BEG to apply for a Card of Membership in the BOYS' BRIGADE, and in doing so I agree to comply with the Rules of the Brigade, and desire to be true to Christ in my life, and to help other boys to be so.

Full Name, Hugh Mackenzie

Address, 15 Park Terrace Lane

Age last Birthday, 14 years

Date of Birthday, 7th february

Teacher's Name, Mr Gillies

The above Form is to be filled up by every boy who wishes to be enrolled as a Member, and handed in at the next meeting of the Brigade, along with one penny as the cost of the Membership Card. 1 6

[J. Cooper]

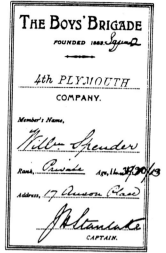

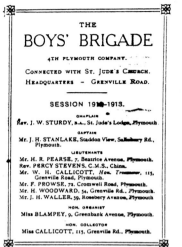

Band Master:
Mr. A. LEE
Deputy Band Master:
Mr. W. FOLLAND

Non-Commissioned Officers:
Staff-Sergeants—F. SKELLY, W. LUXTON, W. STIBBS,
V. H. GRADDON, R. LANGWORTHY
Drum-Major—W. LEACH
Colour-Sergeant—G. R. SALTER
Sergeant Fifer—S. SKELLY
Sergeant-Drummer—C. HOSKING
Company-Sergeants—G. LUSH, W. HAYWARD
Corporals—R. POLMEAR (Drums), G. WOODWARD,
G. LEWIS (Fifes), J. HOSKING (Bugles)
NICHOLLS
Lance-Corporals—W. TONKIN (Drums), R. ROWSE, W.
VEALE, W. S. ADAMS, C. COOMBES, J. DOW
(Fifes), W. GRIFFITH (Bugles)

Weekly Meetings are held as under (subject to alterations
as circumstances may demand)
Sunday—Bible Class. Headquarters. 3 p.m.
Gospel Service, Churchroom. 6-30 p.m.
Non-Commissioned Officers' Meeting, last Sunday in each
month, 8 p.m.
Monday—Band Practice
Tuesday—Reading Room, Special Classes or Meetings. Hand-
Bell Practices
Wednesday—Company Drill, Route Marches, &c.
Thursday—Gymnasium open 7-30 p.m.
Friday—Ambulance Class. Reading and Games Room
Saturday—Afternoon Rambles and Bathing during summer
months. Football during the season

THE BOYS' BRIGADE
4TH PLYMOUTH COMPANY
Connected with St. Jude's Church.

RULES.

1.—Members must be Boys between 12 and 17 years of age.
2.—Every Member must be a total abstainer, and is strictly forbidden to smoke.
3.—Members must at all times set an example of good conduct to their Comrades and other Boys, and conduct themselves in a quiet and orderly manner, when going to and from Parade, Church, or other Meeting.
4.—Members must come on Parade in Uniform, sharp to the hour, looking smart and clean.
5.—Members must give prompt and cheerful obedience to all the orders of their Officers and Non-Commissioned Officers.
6.—Members must always salute their Officers when they meet them, or go up to address them, either on or off parade, and will always use "Sir," when addressing an Officer. Boys in Uniform will salute Officers of other Companies in Uniform.
7.—During Drill there must be strict attention, and no talking in the ranks except when "standing easy." In Church there must be quietness and attention, and perfect reverence at all times.
8.—Any member who misses two consecutive Meetings (Drill or Church), without good and satisfactory reason, is liable to be struck off the Roll.

9.—Any Member changing his address will at once intimate the change, *in writing*, to the Captain of the Company.
10.—Members will be held responsible for making themselves acquainted with these Rules and with all the Orders posted on the Company Notice Board, and for giving attention to all intimations made at Drill or Bible Class.
These Rules will be strictly enforced.

The Officers Expect every Boy

To read every day the portion of Scripture laid down in the Boys' Brigade Scripture Union Card, and to remember his prayers morning and evening.
Never to use bad language
Always to prefer DUTY to either pleasure or inclination.
Always to endeavour to maintain the purity, kindliness, courtesy, and mutual confidence that should prevail in a Company of The Boys' Brigade.
At all times and in all places to maintain the honour of the "4TH PLYMOUTH," and to remember that the credit of the Boys' Brigade is in the keeping of every individual Member of the Company.
Remember, Boys, your Officers wish to be your *friends.* Be frank and open with them, and do not hesitate to come to them if ever you are in trouble or difficulty.

JOHN H. STANLAKE, *Captain,*
STADDON VIEW,
SALISBURY ROAD, PLYMOUTH.

There is no Entrance Fee or Subscription to the Company, but every boy on joining must purchase a Cap (with number), Belt, and Haversack, which shall be his property, but this uniform is only to be worn for parades or "orderly" duty.

The following attractions are organised for the use of members:—

Drum and Fife and Bugle Band.—Fee 2d. per week, to be paid whether present or not. Boys who are regular in their payments, will at certain intervals, be entitled to a bonus should the receipts be more than sufficient to cover the cost of instruction.

Company Entertainments
Ambulance - - - - -
Swimming - - - - -
Hand-Bell Ringing - - -
Signalling Instruction - -
Gymnasium - - - - -   FREE to members, but
Physical Training - - -   boys to pay for any
Harriers - - - - - -   necessary personal
Football - - - - - -   equipment.
Reading and Games Room -
Savings Bank - - - -
Company Camp
Afternoon Rambles and Picnics.
Bank Holiday Outings.

AWARDS.

A Squad Challenge Medal is awarded to the N.C.O. in charge of the squad obtaining the highest percentage of attendance marks, to be worn by him during the month following that in which it has been won. The N.C.O. who succeeds in winning it the greatest number of times during the session will be presented with a Medal as his own property.

Prizes.—Bibles, Books, Silver Pins, or other articles at the discretion of the Officers—will be awarded to boys who obtain the highest number of marks during the session. To obtain a full attendance mark, boys must be present in correct uniform as ordered.

Three Years' Service Anchors,
Sergeants' Proficiency Stars,
N.C.O.'s Certificates of Proficiency
One Year Efficiency Badges,
Ambulance Certificates.
} Awarded in accordance with rules laid down in the B.B. Manual.

Discharge Certificates are presented to all boys who, on leaving the Company have served in the B.B. at least three years with good conduct.

Other prizes will be awarded for special occasions as may be announced.

COMPANY HONOURS.

Drum and Fife Band awarded first place in the Plymouth, Devonport and Stonehouse Battalion: 1906, 1907, 1909, 1910, 1911, and 1912. Bugle Band first in 1908, 1909, 1910, 1911, and 1912: Band selected to play at the Camp of the Waterford Company at Tramore, Ireland, 1906: Hand-Bell Ringers selected to perform at the Brigade Demonstration, Royal Albert Hall, London, 1906: Battalion Trophy for Swimming won 1906, and 1912: Battalion Trophy for Drill won 1909, 1910, and 1912: Battalion First-aid Trophy won 1910, 1911, and 1912: Football Trophy won 1912.

The Company supports a Cot at Pakhoi, South China, in connection with the C.M.S. Medical Mission.

Attendance is not compulsory at the Sunday evening services and at Drill, and while it is not obligatory on members to join the Band or other adjunct of the Company, should they do so it can be only on condition that they will be regular and punctual in their attendances at all meetings and practices. Leave will only be granted in very special cases.

Boys not regularly attending other Schools on Sunday afternoons are expected to join the Company Bible Class or St. Jude's Schools.

Except in special cases, meetings are over by 9-30 p.m.

Motto for the Year:
"Quit you like men; be strong"

THE BOYS' BRIGADE.

Extracts from the Constitution.

"The Object of the Brigade shall be the advancement of Christ's Kingdom among Boys, and the promotion of habits of Obedience, Reverence, Discipline, Self-respect, and all that tends towards a true Christian Manliness.

"Military Organisation and Drill shall be used as a means of securing the interest of the Boys, banding them together in the work of the Brigade, and promoting among them such habits as the Brigade is designed to form.

"Boys between the ages of 12 and 17 shall be eligible for Enrolment as Members of the Brigade, and may remain Members until the end of the Session in which they become 17. In applying for Enrolment they shall fill up a Form of Application, agreeing to comply with the Rules of the Company, and to set an example of Good Conduct to their Comrades and other Boys. Members shall do all they can to further the Object of the Brigade.

"Strict Discipline and Obedience shall be enforced by all Officers."

4th Plymouth Coy. B.B. Membership Card Session 1912-13

Family Group c1910.

A rare glimpse of BB Boys at home with their family. In late Victorian and Edwardian times families were usually large, whereas houses, even for skilled workers, were small. This somewhat cramped picture taken in the back garden illustrates typical clothing of the day. The Boys are wearing, with their Brigade equipment, large white collars, ribbons, and Norfolk jackets. Dad is wearing his suit, tie and Cap! Hats are compulsory for the ladies too.

Brigade membership gave Boys the chance to escape from the restricted space of their home environment and involve themselves in activities which could not be contemplated alongside the practical household necessities of eating, sleeping and washing.

'Off Duty'.

Another Valentines Postcard reflecting a 'social' aspect of Brigade life. The picture was taken in Baxter Park, Dundee c1906. The Brigade Boys are the ones who 'get the girls'... or should it be 'lasses'?

H.R.H. The Prince of Wales, Inspects 1st Newport. c1920.

The first Boys' Brigade Company in Wales was the 1st Newport, founded by George Reynolds, a local draper who had worked in Glasgow and taught at the North Woodside Mission Sunday School. It was formed in 1887 at Havelock Street Presbyterian Church.

THE CHURCH LADS' BRIGADE
&
LONDON DIOCESAN CHURCH LADS' BRIGADE

C.L.B. 1891-1978   L.D.C.L.B. 1891-1919

Object: *CLB '...the advancement of Christ's Kingdom among Church lads of all classes, the promotion of charity, reverence, patriotism, discipline, self-respect, and all that tends towards true Christian manliness.'*

Motto: CLB: 'Fight the Good Fight'   LDCLB: 'I Serve'

The Church Lads' Brigade was founded on 11th November 1891 in Fulham by Walter Mallock Gee. (He had been running the Co. since July 23rd). Like William Smith, Gee was a keen member of the 'Volunteers' as well as being full time secretary of the Church of England Temperance Society (Junior Division). The Temperance 'Bands of Hope' were not enough, in his opinion, to hold the older Lad.

Many Sectarian 'Boys Brigades' were proposed at the end of the 19th Century but few were as successful as Gee's Anglican CLB; even then, its start was bifurcated as the result of an argument between Temperance and Total abstinence. Dr Temple, Archbishop of London in 1891, was in favour of a Total abstinence CLB; so much so that he authorised the formation of the 'London Diocesan CLB'. The founder and first Commandant was Everard Ford. In 1918 Cadet-Colonel Everard Ford O.B.E. retired after 27 years in command. This separatist organisation remained independent until 1919 when it re-united with the CLB still retaining its own constitution and regulations.

The Badge of the CLB is emblematical of that part of the Epistle of Paul to the Ephesians which refers to the 'Whole armour of God'.

From one Company in 1891 growth was rapid. By 1893 the CLB was represented in every English Diocese except Ely. It had spread overseas by 1894 although it was never strong in Scotland.

Development of the C.L.B., from the start, was along 'centralist' lines. Much more militaristic than the B.B. it came as no surprise when, in 1911 it affiliated wholesale to the Government's Cadet Scheme. Hundreds of its members died in the Great War, many on the Somme in 1916. These Lads were members of the two Battalions of the King's Royal Rifle Corps composed entirely of CLB members & ex-members. The London Diocesan C.L.B. entered the Cadet Scheme on May 11th 1911 as the 'Church Cadet Brigade' becoming the largest single recognised body in Britain.

In the late inter-war period C.L.B. numbers dropped dramatically. In 1936 there was a complete re-organization with the Brigade returning to less militaristic methods as originally intended.

A shorter version of the 'object' came into use after 1936.

A Beautiful 'Undivided back' Postcard produced by the C.L.B. Headquarters c1902.

The C.L.B. was quick to spread into the Empire. By 1892 there was a Company at St. John's in Newfoundland, but unfortunately fire is reported to have 'destroyed its resources' that year, leading to it being supported by Lads in England. The English Lads sent '50 Equipments' to their North American comrades. By 1894 South Africa and the West Indies were a part of the overseas C.L.B. Family.

Described in 1911 as 'Imperial energy' the expansion of the C.L.B. went hand in hand with the expansion of Empire.

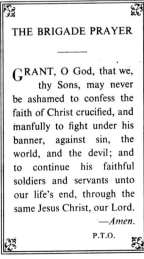

THE BRIGADE PRAYER

GRANT, O God, that we, thy Sons, may never be ashamed to confess the faith of Christ crucified, and manfully to fight under his banner, against sin, the world, and the devil; and to continue his faithful soldiers and servants unto our life's end, through the same Jesus Christ, our Lord.

—Amen.

P.T.O.

Published by the Church Lads' Brigade,
58, Gloucester Place, London, W.1.

A C.L.B. Sgt. from Louth (Lincs) c1908   **Lad's Prayer Card**

C.L.B. UNIFORM v EQUIPMENT

Lads in the early C.L.B. Companies, wearing their 'Equipment' in public had called forth much ridicule. 'Roughs' threw stones and mud and 'picketed' the drill room of the original Fulham Coy 'Terrorising the smaller lads". From the start, the C.L.B. Leaders were determined that their equipment would be the best. 'Better quality than used in The Boys' Brigade' was their boast. Officers were encouraged to wear 'Full equipment' as an example to the Boys and not just a cap like the BB Officers.

'Equipment' for the C.L.B. Lad consisted of a Forage Cap with yellow braid and metal badge, Haversack & or Leather crossbelt, Leather Waist Belt and armband. Full uniform was, at the outset of the C.L.B., considered to be too much like the military or 'volunteers'. All the Brigades faced a barrage of criticism from the anti-militarists in the Churches. The 'Halfway House' arrangement was not only cheaper than a full uniform but it enabled the Officers to keep a check on the everyday working clothes of the Boy. Only after the 1st World War did 'full' uniform emerge as a regular viable alternative in the C.L.B. as a response to Khaki uniforms worn at the end of Government Cadet affiliation. Other organizations such as the BB, BLB, & JLB were also introducing full uniforms at that time.

The Catholic BB & London Diocesan C.L.B. had full uniforms as standard with 'Equipment' as the alternative.

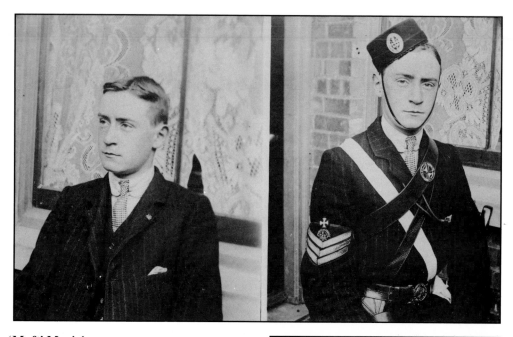

'Mufti Magic'

This unusual split-photo card shows a CLB Sgt in his normal 'mufti' suit, and at the same time wearing his 'Equipment' over the top! In addition he is wearing a carrying holster for the Co. Colour.

Look after them, plenty of light, water and food and they grow bigger each day!

14

FORMALITY

Benwell Co. 1st Newcastle Batt. c1910
By the time this Photographic Card was produced there was very little 'stigma' attached to wearing C.L.B. Equipment ... quite the opposite, indeed the two young lads wearing boaters and peering over the fence, seem somewhat in awe.

& INFORMALITY

'Hedgehogs'

Pond Life

Beside the seaside

"Oh Mr Porter"

Grimsby (St. John's) C.L.B. Co. 2409

15

THE DEVELOPMENT OF THE CLB UNIFORM

This Company illustrates well the changes in the C.L.B. Uniform from its start until well into the 1930's.

Grimsby Littlecoats Co. C.L.B. 1910

The Lads are wearing the original standard equipment as they parade outside their tent at the Saltburn Camp with their Chaplain Rev. Feltrum Fagin.

1916

By 1916, five years into the Governments Cadet Scheme, the whole group are kitted out in khaki. They have lost their identity as a Church organisation to become in every respect 'cadets'. The Cadet Grant was withdrawn in 1923 and the Grimsby Littlecoats like the rest of the CLB (who had survived the war) returned to their roots of nineteen years earlier, but not to the earlier uniform style.

1930s

Seen here in the 1930's they are resplendent in their new full Blue Uniforms. White hat covers are being worn. The only continuity from 1910 seems to be a rather older looking Rev Feltrum Fagin!

[Neville Gray]

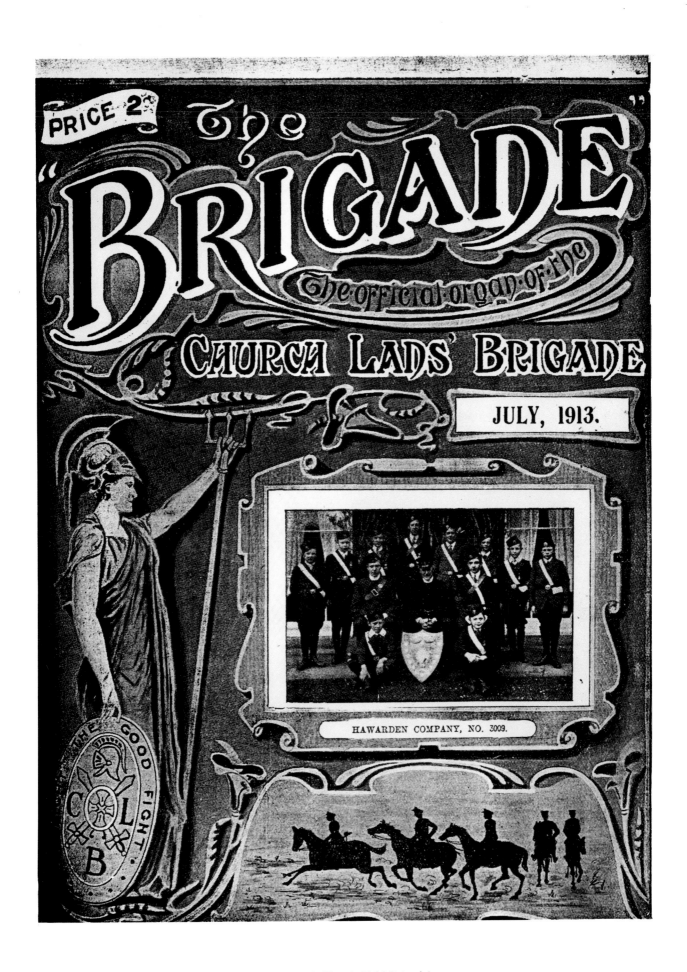

[Church Lads' & Church Girls' Brigade]

17

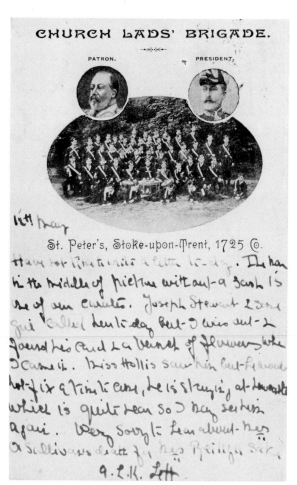

Church Lads' Brigade "Review Series," No. 3

CORONATION REVIEW.   THE MUSTER AT WELLINGTON BARRACKS, LONDON.

His Royal Highness the Prince of Wales reviewed the C.L.B. on the occasion of his father's Coronation. Shortly after which His Majesty King Edward VII consented to become the Patron of the C.L.B. as he did other Brigades. Subsequent sovereigns have also consented to give their patronage to the Brigades.

On this occasion, the turnout of the Lads was regarded as particularly good, a fact attributed to the system of supplying uniform 'on issue' from Headquarters. Boys would be charged at the rate of two shillings (10p) each. One shilling and sixpence (7^1/$_2$p) for equipment and sixpence (2^1/$_2$p) for 'capitation'. This Picture postcard published, no doubt with pride, by C.L.B. HQ. was part of the second 'Review Series' which included reviews in Rochester & Lichfield. The earlier series included the Diamond Jubilee review in Hyde Park 1897.

CHURCH LADS' BRIGADE.

PATRON.   PRESIDENT.

St. Peter's, Stoke-upon-Trent, 1725 Co.

CHURCH LADS' BRIGADE.

PATRON.   PRESIDENT.

St. Aidan's (Newcastle-on-Tyne) Company No. 694.

"Undivided Back" Postcards. C.L.B. St. Peter's Stoke-upon-Trent & St. Aidan's, Newcastle-on-Tyne.

Standard sized postcards were introduced in 1899 but the back had to be used for the address alone. Some space had to be left on the 'front' for a message. In January 1902 the Post Office regulations were altered allowing messages to be written on the back, separated from the address by a vertical line.

The St. Peters' card was posted on 12th May 1904, no doubt using up some of the old stock. Miss Lett is writing to her father, or brother? Rev Canon Lett in Ireland.

The President of the C.L.B. (1892-1942) was Field Marshal H.R.H. The Duke of Connaught & Strathearn K.G. K.T.

In the C.L.B., Companies were numbered nationally, in order of foundation rather than by locality such as in the Boys' Brigade. Co. No. 1725 could be further identified by giving its town and Church Connection. Co. No 694 is the elder of the two.

[Stephen Lane]

London Diocesan C.L.B. c1910 & c1917

The full Dark Blue tunic uniform with its scarlet piping of the L.D.C.L.B. can be clearly seen on these two pictures. The earlier picture shows the Lads wearing the Forage Cap with Scarlet Band. (Note the lack of large oval badge). On the later one, prior to the amalgamation with the rest of the C.L.B., the hats have changed to the military pattern peaked cap, retaining their distinctive scarlet band, setting the style for the rest of the Brigade some twenty years later.

Perhaps the most striking feature of both pictures is the obvious lack of poverty.

c1917

c1910

19

THE JEWISH LADS' BRIGADE

Object: *To instil into the Rising Generation from its earliest youth, habits of Orderliness, Cleanliness, and Honour, so that in learning to respect themselves, they will do credit to their Community.*

Motto: 'They go from strength to strength'.

1895-1974

The Jewish Lads' Brigade was founded in 1895 by Albert Edward Goldsmid, a self-declared 'nationalist Jew' and the British Chief of 'Chovevi Zion'. As a Zionist Anglophile he made a successful career as a Staff Officer in the British Army. Whilst Colonel-In-Command at Cardiff he inspected the local C.L.B. and commented "Something similar should be arranged for our Jewish Lads". He soon became a Vice-President of the C.L.B. Naturally, it was not long before he decided to form the J.L.B., his recruits coming from the sons of Jewish Immigrants crowding into the East End Ghettoes of London. His aim was to help the poor Jewish Boys particularly between the time they left school and the time they became old enough to join the Jewish Working Mens Clubs.

Goldsmid, with support from the Maccabeans held his first meeting in February 1895 in the hall of the Jews Free School in Spitalfields. By the 1900's with the gradual dispersal of the Jewish community, the J.L.B. then numbering perhaps 4,000 spread out into other areas of London and the U.K. Units were also formed in Canada and S. Africa. One of the early problems was that Officers from upper middle class Anglo-Jewish families often found the need for an Interpreter when talking to the Boys' Russian & Polish parents! When the Officer had gone the Parents would turn to the Boy and exclaim.. 'and he's a Jew?'

A lasting function of the J.L.B. was to facilitate racial integration and 'lift' the ghetto youth into the mould of the English Public School.

Given the background, it is not surprising that the J.L.B. were quick to affiliate with the Government's Cadet Scheme. 23 members, under the Command of Col. Goldsmid enlisted to serve in the Boer War, 535 members were killed in the First War and many in the Second World War. In the inter-war period of the '20's and '30's the J.L.B. continued their affiliation to the Cadet Scheme in the face of a general increase in pacifism and the 'opting out' of other voluntary Brigades. During the Second War the J.L.B. virtually ceased operations. In the Post-War period the J.L.B. have continued a more militaristic approach than the other Brigades, retaining links with the Army Cadet Force.

In 1974 the J.L.B. joined together with the Jewish Girls' Brigade to form the "Jewish Lads and Girls Brigade".

[The Jewish Lads' & Girls' Brigade]

[The Jewish Lads' and Girls' Brigade]

Col. Goldsmid, founder of the J.L.B. modelled his uniforms very closely upon those of the C.L.B., which had been his inspiration. In most respects, even on close examination, it would be hard to tell them apart from C.L.B. Lads. Even the Officers uniforms followed the C.L.B. pattern.

The Boys were under very close scrutiny, it seems, in 1902, when at the Sandhills Camp a census was carried out by the Royal Commission on Alien Immigration. It was found that over seventy five percent of the Boys were of foreign parentage and many of them had been born abroad, but 'they looked just like English Boys… That is most remarkable'

[The Jewish Lads' and Girls' Brigade]

21

From the *Jewish World.*   1
Jewish Lads' Brigade Display at Queen's Hall.

[The Jewish Lads' and Girls' Brigade]

Birmingham Jewish Lads' Brigade c1921

[R. Kaplan]

Some of the strongest J.L.B. Companies were in the Provinces, Manchester, Glasgow, and Birmingham in particular. These Birmingham Boys are pictured outside the 'Singer's Hill' Synagogue under their Commanding Officer Col. 'Bunny' Solomon. This Real Photographic Post Card was produced by L.H. Drapkin of B'ham. Louis Drapkin is the Sgt. Major fourth from the right, second row up, he produced many photographs of the Birmingham J.L.B. The superb trophy is probably the Prince of Wales's Boxing Shield, a source of great pride in Birmingham and the result of intense National inter-cadet rivalry and competition.

The J.L.B. were amongst the first youth organizations to be incorporated into the Government's Cadet Scheme, spending a long time in khaki.

Birmingham J.L.B. Trophies gained at camp 1929 in Blackpool.

[R. Kaplan]

[R. Kaplan]

Camp 1928. Birmingham J.L.B. Deganwy.
This lorry owned by J.W. Owen & Hughes Ltd loaded with camp kit, forms a background for Charlie Hoff, Lew Morris, Eppie Friedmann and friends.

CATHOLIC BOYS' BRIGADE

1896-c1959

Object: *'To safeguard the Faith and Morals of our Catholic Lads, when they leave school'*

Motto: 'Ne Cede Malis' (Be not overcome by evil).

The Catholic Boys' Brigade was founded in September 1896 by Rev. Father Felix Segesser, a young Assistant Priest at the Dockhead Students Institute Boys' Club in Bermondsey S.E. London. Fr. Segesser was concerned about keeping together the working Lads of his Mission in the years immediately after they left school. He was also concerned that they might lose the Faith. He hit on the idea of forming 'Cadets' and saw in this idea the solution to his problem. The original name was the 'South London Catholic Brigade' named after the existing 'South London Catholic League'. Some older Lads were still wearing 'SLCB' shoulder titles as late as 1905.

Like many of the founders of the Brigades, Fr Segesser had not envisaged the growth of the organization, even outside his own Parish. At first it spread within the confines of East London with Fr. Newton at Rotherhithe starting the second Company.

The emblem of the CBB was an eight pointed star with the papal insignia and motto taken from St Paul.

Existing Catholic Guilds and Boys Clubs were regarded by Segesser as 'Dismal Failures'. He said that Clubs appealed to the Boys love of pleasure and amusement but lacked the discipline necessary to the successful management of Boys.

In 1909 His Holiness Pope Pius X specially blessed the colours of the CBB and His Grace the Archbishop of Westminster provided a Constitution.

Although resisting the Govt. for years the C.B.B. eventually went into the Territorial Cadet Force. Companies and Battalions entered at different times between 1913-27: eg. Bradford 10.6.13, Leeds 10.6.13, Liverpool 1.6.14, Westminster 19.10.14 and Salford 14.2.19. Company losses came not only from War casualties but also from financial hardship when the Govt. Cadet cash was withdrawn at the end of the scheme. By the 1920's & '30's some new units were starting up however. Salford had at least 22 Coys in 1921. Some C.B.B. Companies decided to stay in the Cadet Force, dropping their 'C.B.B.' Title to become 'Catholic Cadets'. eg. Coventry (1918), Westminster (1919), Walsall (1920).

It was perhaps the C.B.B.'s relationship with, and accommodation of, Scouting that caused its eventual demise in the remaining strongholds such as Salford after the First War. From the earliest days of Scouting Fr Segesser had seen no problems with C.B.B. Boys being in both the C.B.B. & the B.P. Scouts.

The Inter-War period was one of increased competition from Pacifist movements and alienation of units in the New Republic of Ireland. Only a few C.B.B. Bands were able to survive the post Second world war decline in all Brigades, although some were still operating in Lancashire as recently as 1959. Perhaps with a life of 64 yrs it is unfair to call the C.B.B. 'short-lived'; The Salesian BB (With two Companies) is still in existence in Malta!

Exact figures are difficult to determine but by c1910 the C.B.B. had 118 Companies grouped into 14 Battalions from the original No 1 at Southwark through to No 14 in Edinburgh. Later, more Battalions were added with No 18 being the 'Salesian B.B.' in Malta. (Three Companies). By 1913 there was a Battalion in Bradford, possibly No 19. The C.B.B. in Ireland had its own Brigade and Battalion organization. From around 1918 the Salford Battalion seems to have been operating Independently as the 'Salford Diocesan C.B.B.'

The Battalions of the Catholic Boys' Brigade (1912)

1. Southwark
2. Westminster
3. Leeds
4. Newport (Gwent)
5. Salford
6. Nottingham
7. Hexham/Newcastle
8. Liverpool
9. Shrewsbury
10. South Staffs (Inc. N. B'ham.)
11. Portsmouth
12. North Staffs
13. Warwickshire (Inc. S. B'ham.)
14. Edinburgh
15. Glasgow
16. Aberdeen (Later merged with Glasgow)
17. Plymouth
18. Malta (Salesian B.B.)

Entered at Stationers' Hall.   Price 1d.

[Roman Catholic Church. Archdiocese of Southwark]

The C.B.B. adopted a full uniform from the outset, consisting: Green tunic (Cost 8s 6d in 1910) and trousers (6s 6d), green forage cap worn either with or without badge, distinctive white belt and haversack. Collar badges were worn on tunic. Marching boots were obtainable from H.Q. price 4s 9d and carbines 7s. Due to the 'high cost' the full uniform was optional but encouraged because *'It wrote the word "Catholic" on the Boy'* Green for Ireland with Red trimmings representing England was the colour scheme chosen for Caps, Tunics & trousers. A smart, bright colourful uniform, introduced only after Fr Segesser had reluctantly lost his battle in favour of a more flamboyant 'Zouaves' uniform similar to that worn by the Papal Guard.'

[Roman Catholic Church. Archdiocese of Southwark]

Holy Name C.B.B. Co. Manchester c1912.
Holy name Co. met in the school yard and volunteer hall every night of the week! The Capt was T.H. Walker Lt's were W. Harkins, R. Halliday & Dockney. In 1912 there were 180 Boys on roll.

Extract from the 1908 Annual Report of the C.B.B., on 'The Formation of a new C.B.B. Company'

'...and so by degrees the Company takes shape, develops, enlarges its activities and finally one great day, stands upon parade at the door of the church, complete in all respects. A drum-Major with his mace leads these hundred Catholic Boys; behind him the fife and bugle band with drums and cymbals, then the Captain with his escort and the main body in regular order of fours flanked by subalterns and sergeants, and in the rear the Ambulance with stretcher, haversack and water bottle, and possibly cyclists or other squads. It is a living, breathing, sentient and very vigorous thing this Company of ours. It stands for all that is best and noblest in Catholic young manhood. It cries aloud its loyalty to God's Vicar on earth. It enters the church as a compact body, witnessing to the faith that is in it. It approaches the Sacraments as a Company, edifying priests and people and setting an example to those who will soon be recruits to it. It sends forth into every-day life and toil and the work which is a blessed thing, a hundred steady, honourable, self-respecting members of society who glory in the name of Catholic'.

Edmonton C.B.B. Co. London. c1910.
Note the papal insignia on the Bass Drum

Catholic Boys' Brigade Camp, Effingham, Surrey.

[Roman Catholic Church Archdiocese of Southwark]

Postcard from Fr. F Segesser – Founder of the Catholic Boys' Brigade
This postcard was sent to Mr. C.H. Nicholls on July 19th 1905 and posted in Deptford. At this time 'Mr' Nicholls was a general supplier to the C.B.B. and maker of steel name punches. (The type used to mark rifles etc). Fr Segesser had 'recruited' him to substitute as a member of the Quartermaster's staff and mentions that he has his certificate as an Officer. Obviously Fr Segesser had received a letter 'full of good sense suggestions' from Nicholls. 'Lt' Nicholls was to assist Lt Johnson due to the absence of Capt Statter. Fr Segesser writes. . 'so glad you are coming in uniform'

'Major' Nicholls went on to become the Brigade's National Quartermaster based at their headquarters in the Bishop's House, Southwark, S.E.

THE BOYS' LIFE BRIGADE

1899 – 1926

Object: *'The objects of the Brigade are to lead our Boys to the service of Christ; to train them for an active, disciplined and useful manhood; to promote habits of self-respect, obedience, courtesy and helpfulness to others, and all that makes for a manly, Christian character'*

Motto: 'To save Life'

The Boys' Life Brigade was founded in the autumn of 1899 by Dr John Brown Paton, under the auspices of the National Sunday School Union. Dr Paton was the influential, recently retired, Principal of the Nottingham Congregational Institute. Born in Galston Ayrshire in 1830, the son of a hand-loom weaver and small shopkeeper, he lived most of his life in England after becoming a Congregational Minister.

Paton persuaded the N.S.S.U. to adopt the B.L.B. method with an emphasis on Life-Saving (from Fire & Water) as a substitute for military drill. Like many non-conformists he disliked the military methods employed by The Boys' Brigade, the 'model' rifle being the object of particular criticism.

The first Company was formed by a Major C.R. Woodward in Nottingham and was known as the 'Paton' Coy. The organisation spread rapidly, outnumbering the B.B. in many places... including London.

The Junior organization was known from 1920 as 'The Lifeboys'.

A four-sided programme was followed, based upon mental, physical, devotional & social development.

By 1913 the BB & BLB were talking about Union; after all, objects, uniform and organization were similar. The affiliation of some BB Coys to the Govt. Cadet Scheme kept the organizations apart until thirteen years later. From 1st October 1926 the Union of the BLB and BB took place along with the Junior organizations of each. Numbers were as follows: BB (Over 11 yrs) 70,390. BLB (Over 11 yrs) 20,977.

A Letter written by a proud B.L.B. Boy (and prospective Sgt.). Manchester, October 1912.

Dear Sir,

We've had a ripping Church Parade here for the B.L.B. Officers' Annual Meetings. Two Battalions, eight bands, and three colour parties turned out – about 600 altogether, I should say. When we moved off the column looked fine.

The Church was full up when we had all got into our seats. There were rows and rows of B.L.B. chaps in review order, and their white haversacks and shiny belts showed up fine in the sunshine. The Sergeant's red sashes stood out ripping against the other kids' uniforms. I reckon a sergeant looks all right in full dress.

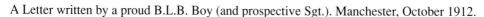

Rev. S.F. Collier, the Battalion Chaplain, preached, and Sir Francis Belsey read. We had real decent hymns; not girls' hymns, but ones a chap could let go his voice over. I reckon we nearly shook the roof. The drums and colours were piled up in front of the pulpit. I believe they boomed like as if they were being hit when we sang some of the hymns.

Yours Faithfully,
Walter Curtis
Corporal, B.L.B.

A B.L.B. Company c1908

The close sartorial similarity between the B.L.B. and their progenitor the Boys' Brigade can be clearly seen here. A Stiff navy blue forage cap (Pill Box) is worn; displaying, in most cases, the Coy Number with two narrow rows of magenta braid a magenta button on top and red cloth cross at the front. A black leather belt with white canvas haversack usually worn over the right shoulder emphasises the similarity with the other Brigades. The Sgt's on this picture are wearing a Red sash over the right shoulder with the white haversack worn over the left. Staff Sgts and Officers are wearing a leather cross belt over the left shoulder. Black belts and Red Sashes continued through the change to full uniform and were used as an alternative after union with the Boys' Brigade. Note the lack of model Rifles!

'Our House' B.L.B. Boy & Sister.
Kings Heath, Birmingham 1907

A B.L.B. Drummer. 28th London (Tooting) Coy.

29

9th Manchester Coy. B.L.B. at Abergele c1922

Some of these Boys are wearing the new B.L.B. alternative Full Uniform introduced in 1918 and consisting; navy blue tunic trimmed with magenta on the collar. White shoulder lanyard, magenta tie, navy blue shorts, dark stockings with red stripe in tops along with the haversack and black belt. Boys over 14 yrs, like the Sgts & Staff Sgts seen here, could wear navy blue knee breeches with magenta piping and puttees. The field-service cap had, by this time, replaced the forage cap completely. It was the B.L.B. influence which introduced a field service cap option to the united B.B./B.L.B. from 1926.

A B.L.B. (& G.L.B.) Company in 1922.

Postcard by Bennett Clark of Wolverhampton. The Boys' & officers full uniforms can be clearly seen.

Follow the Christ the King

A Picture postcard published by the B.L.B. H.Q. c1920. The full uniform can be clearly seen in the painting of the Boys.

[Drawings: Reproduced with the kind permission of the Brigade Sec. of The Boys Brigade]

[J. Cooper]

2. STARS AND STRIPES

Rewards have always produced results from Boys. The whole quasi-military structure depended upon these incentives. Non-Commissioned Officers were, perhaps, the Brigade's backbone and the chief means by which a sense of 'esprit-de-corps' was fostered within the Company unit.

As a 'Non-Com' a member held a position of responsibility and with it much status and respect; naturally, many Boys were far more keen on the latter than the former. Promotion was not really intended to be a reward, but working to gain a stripe was a great incentive.

Some of the first B.B. Badges were 'stars' awarded from 1887 by a few Battalions. Most of the Brigades had awards for efficiency, service and proficiency from the outset. Like stripes, badges could be worn on the arm, a clear expression of merit and achievement.

Catholic B.B. Boys could gain promotion stripes, good conduct-stripes, gilt and silver stars for regular attendance along with proficiency badges for ambulance, signallers, cyclists, drummer, bugler, armourer and pioneer.

Members of the Boys' Own Brigade could qualify for a three year 'Good conduct' star.

[Reproduced with the kind permission of the Brigade Secretary of The Boys' Brigade.]

THE BOYS' BRIGADE BADGES c1923

The Boys' Brigade started the system of proficiency Badges in 1889 with the introduction of the Ambulance Badge, a larger version of the one pictured in the bottom left hand corner of this Informative Brigade Picture Postcard from the early 1920's.

The idea of 'Service' Badges had been introduced a year earlier with the 'three year' service Anchor. It was 1904 before the one year efficiency badge was introduced.

The 'Buttonhole' Badge appeared in 1911 for use out of uniform (or in – uniform from 1918).

The King's Badge instituted in 1913 by permission of H.M. King George V was the premier B.B. award; the first being presented to Col/Sgt Arthur Reid of the 1st Glasgow Coy. in March 1914.

'Old Boys' had a special badge for wear on the watch chain, introduced in 1907.

The Cross For Heroism was introduced on 1st Sept. 1902 and first awarded in October 1904/ (Only 191 awarded to date). It is worn on the left breast.

Other proficiency awards remained unchanged until 1927 when the emblem was altered to accommodate the B.L.B. Cross motif.

The Scouts Badge, introduced in 1909 had silver and gold varieties (1st & 2nd class) but was discontinued completely in 1927.

Proficiency badges were worn on the right arm, with The King's Badge on the left. The 1914/18 National Service Badge was worn below the Kings Badge. The 1939/45 National Service Badge was worn on the right arm.

Six new proficiency badges were issued from 1927-1945, with a further four between 1946-68.

Adverts from the C.B.B. Gazette
[Roman Catholic Church, Archdiocese of Southwark]

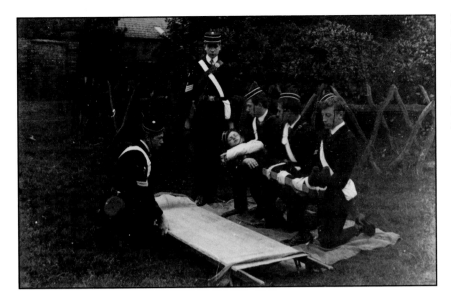

N.C.O.'s of the 2nd Rugby Company Boys' Brigade earning their Ambulance Badges. c1914.

Captain Faulkner sent this P.C. to thank Mrs Cleaver for her help at the Rummage Sale where £6 clear profit was made!

Senior C.L.B. NCO's at Camp c1908.

Note the Swagger Canes and lack of proficiency badges. The lad standing (end right) is wearing a 'Camp Police' armlet. Medals were awarded for C.L.B. service rather than badges.

Officers & N.C.O.'s of Co. No. 62. St. Austin's Stafford Catholic Boys' Brigade.

The New N.C.O.

L/Cpl Paul Alfred James of the 1st Worthing Coy Boys' Brigade proudly displays his non-commissioned officer's appointment certificate. Dated May 11th 1911. Becoming an N.C.O. meant something special in most Boys' Brigade Companies and the Certificate was certainly worth the trouble!

L/Cpl James has other 'spoils" with him, two presentation books; one probably a Testament or Bible, the one on the top is Charles Kingsley's 'Westward Ho!' A new brush and swagger cane will, no doubt, add to the smartness expected from a Boy of his rank.

Rather unusual for a B.B. Boy are the five medals, perhaps donned specially for the photograph. One could be a medal celebrating King George's Coronation in June 1911, about the time the photo was taken; the others are probably Sunday School medals.

If the photographer hadn't come up with the idea of tucking the corner of the certificate under the haversack for stability it is doubtful whether it would have been so legible.

Four 'non-coms' of 16th Brighton B.B. c1920

The senior N.C.O. A London B.B. Staff Sergeant c1918

NCO's Flank a L.D.C.L.B. Battalion out for a 'Field Day' c1910
[Alan Bull]

Two Sergeants of the London Diocesan C.L.B.

L.D.C.L.B. Uniforms were generally full tunic style, as can be seen clearly on these photographs. The earlier Sgt. is not wearing a Haversack, a common occurrence at Camp. The Forage Cap with no Badge or Company numbers and leather cross-belt are distinctive. By 1913 the 'Cadet' style peaked cap featuring the mitre badge, has been adopted although the rest of the uniform remains the same.

The 'military' influence within the L.D.C.L.B. as well as in the C.L.B. generally is obvious. Unlike the Boys' Brigade, full military organization methods of instruction and terminology were employed.

By 1906 the L.D.C.L.B. were about 7,000 strong divided into 160 separate companies. The C.L.B. had 1,259 Companies and a membership of 45,000.

c1909

c1913

'Yours Truly L/Cpl White'… 28th London (Tooting) B.L.B. c1916.

L/Cpl White lived in Trevelyan Rd, Tooting and was a keen member of the Boys' Life Brigade 28th London Coy. He is seen on his signed photograph with Bugle & Fife.

At Benfleet Camp 1919

S/Sgt White with a S/Sgt & Warrant Officer all from 4th S.W. London Batt. Camp at Benfleet 1919. Note: The B.L.B. Awards Badges.

Sgt White appears on other pages (in Vol 2) of this book as a member of the 'Tooting All Clear Boys' in 1918 and demonstrating Club Drill. He went on to serve as an Officer in the Company.

THE B.L.B. LANCE CORPORAL. Extract from a B.L.B. Journal. 1912.

The ambition of each Private is to become a Lance-Corporal. Fellows may find the following hints useful in their efforts after promotion.

The two subjects which are fixed to carry the most marks in the examination for the first stripe are those of Squad Drill and First-Aid. In the former subject several points must be remembered… it is necessary to be smart and to have complete command of one's dulcet tones on these trying occasions. A Lad who gives his commands to a squad in a high falsetto or in a humiliated whisper, does not often succeed in obtaining obedience to them.

The distinguishing feature of the B.L.B. is that the first step in promotion is only obtained after a stiff examination in First-Aid. In the practical part of the test fellows should remember to treat their patients as though an actual accident had taken place. Some lads handle their unfortunate cases in so vigorous a manner that, were a real injury under treatment, 'the last state' of the patient would be far 'worse than the first'. Such lads rarely get any marks.

In the B.L.B. L/Cpls were at least 13 yrs of age, Corporals 14 yrs, Sgts 15 yrs and Staff/Sgts 17 yrs.

NCO's of 28th London (Tooting) Coy. B.L.B. c1916.

Note the fine array of awards, badges and medals.

Company Transport

Boys & NCO's of 1st Horsham Coy. Boys' Life Brigade – April 10th, 1914

[Reproduced with the kind permission of the Brigade Secretary of The Boys' Brigade]

"Five Boys"
[But no chocolate in sight!]

L/Cpl Maurice Kaplan, Jewish Lads' Brigade c1916

A Photographic Post Card produced in the studio of Tallis & Woodcock of Gooch St, Birmingham. Young Maurice is looking the 'real soldier' in his Khaki, webbing, puttees and all! Still not old enough here for his Bar-Mitzvah, Maurice was to serve the J.L.B. in Birmingham very well.

As an energetic Quartermaster Sgt in 1933 at a B'ham Boys' Brigade N.C.O.'s dinner to Celebrate that organization's Jubilee, he stood up to propose the toast 'To the Boys' Brigade' on behalf of 'Kindred Organizations'. His toast was received by Capt. Donald Finnemore (Later Sir Donald) who was, no doubt, pleased to hear Maurice emphasise (for the benefit of the press) that they were not, in the Brigades, training for War. Sir Donald had, in the first world war, served with the Ambulance units because of his pacifist beliefs.

Maurice served in the Royal Engineers when war returned to Europe just six years after his speech in Birmingham.

[R. Kaplan]

BOYS' BRIGADE JUBILEE DINNER.

INFLUENCE OF MOVEMENT ON YOUNG PEOPLE.

A healthy and efficient looking band of youths, the N.C.O.s of the Birmingham Battalion of the Boys' Brigade, who held a jubilee dinner at the Cobden Hotel, Birmingham, on Saturday, were both complimented and encouraged to continue their excellent work in the training of the younger boys for the brigade work. The president of the battalion, Captain D. L. Finnemore, was present, as well as the representatives of the Boy Scouts, the Church Lads' Brigade and the Jewish Lads' Brigade. S. Sergt. Barlow, president of the battalion N.C.O.s' council, presided.

The toast of "The Guests" was given by Sergeant Blundell (8th Company), and an old boy of the brigade, Councillor W. T. Wiggins-Davies, now chairman of the Birmingham Juvenile Employment and Welfare Sub-committee, responded. He said he was glad that the boys of to-day were very much like the boys of his boyhood. He reminded the N.C.O.s of the duties they would have to fulfil as life went on, and in asking them to encourage everyone to join a brigade or some such organisation, said

there were 70,000 boys and girls between fourteen and eighteen in Birmingham, and a very large number of them were in no organisation at all. He said the committee with which he was associated did all it could to foster the good spirit found among such organisations, and encouraged young people to join them.

Sergeant Weighall (18th Company) proposed "Kindred Organisations," and Assistant County Commissioner Horne (Birmingham Boy Scouts), in responding, told the boys the work they were doing was of the utmost importance, and the influence they were exerting on younger boys not only helped those boys, but helped themselves.

During the fifty years of the existence of the Boys' Brigade there had been a great improvement in the tone of youth, and that had been due primarily, not to grown-ups, but to leaders such as the N.C.O.s, who had endeavoured to translate ideals into practice.

Lieut.-Colonel A. M. Downing (C.L.B.), who also responded, said the Boys' Brigade was eight years older than the C.L.B., and they were always proud of their elder brother and took the greatest interest in the work of the organisation. He urged them ever to remember their founder, Sir William Smith.

Q.M.S. Kaplan replied for the Jewish Lads' Brigade.

A Pageant to be Produced.

S. Sergt. Kendall (6th Coventry Company) proposed "The Birmingham Battalion," and this was acknowledged by Captain Finnemore, who told the boys of the trust reposed in them, and said no company could go wrong while it had good N.C.O.s. He mentioned that as a wind-up to the jubilee events this year the battalion intended to produce a Boys' Brigade pageant in October, the profits of which would go to the hospitals. Captain Finnemore mentioned that a considerable advance had been made by the Boys' Brigade in the city during the year, and there were now more than sixty companies, above 2,000 boys and practically 300 officers.

"The Boys' Brigade" was proposed by Q.M.S. Kaplan, who discountenanced the idea prevailing among some people that the boys were being trained for fighting. Everyone connected with the movement knew they were not being trained for war but for peace, and how to become good citizens.

Response was made by Captain B. E. White, of Epsom, representing the Brigade Executive, who congratulated the Birmingham Battalion on its position, and particularly on its president.

57th Birmingham Coy. B.B. 1957.

3. IN GOOD COMPANY

To every Brigade Boy there is only one Company...his own. Small or large the 'esprit de corps' engendered inside the group is and was, paramount. However, it must be said that the right people in the right place at the right time have produced Brigade Companies which were 'special' not only to their own Boys but to their Brigade, their town and often their country.

Brigade Companies have existed in all types of location; Tiny Islands, Cricket grounds, Boys' Clubs, Churches, Chapels, Synagogues, Cathedrals, Schools, Orphanages and Military Bases. In fact anywhere there was considered to be a need, was a place for a Brigade Company.

The 'right' people often emerged from the ranks of the good company, ensuring both its success and continuity. In a new century where transportation and movement of workers was to become widespread, those same committed men & women spread the seed of the Brigade far and wide, taking on fresh challenges; which, in Edwardian Britain, were not difficult to find.

ORPHAN HOMES OF SCOTLAND. 2ND/1ST BRIDGE OF WEIR COY. B.B.

The Quarrier's Homes Boys' Brigade Coy was founded in 1906 as part of the Orphan Homes of Scotland School, Bridge of Weir, Scotland. At that time the Homes had been operating for more than thirty years since their foundation by William Quarrier. The headmaster of the school was B.B. Captain. In 1911 it was Mr. J. Gordon Kennedy M.A. who remained as Capt. at least until the 1st World War.

Besides the B.B. Coy a successful Company of the Girls' Guildry operated at the school.

The School was set amidst a complete 'village' occupied by 'families' living in cottages with perhaps 24 Boys per family. and presumably a similar number for girls families. There was no shortage of recruits on site for the Brigade, the Primary School had, in 1911, 1,067 children on the roll including 615 Boys. There was a 'turnover' of about 30% each year, however, making continuity difficult. In 1911 the Coy numbers were reported at: 88 N.C.O.'s & Boys and four Officers rising by one or two each year until 1918. The War put the Company into 'abeyance' although many former pupils visited the school whilst on leave and it was reported that: *'It has been gratifying to learn from their own lips how valuable they found the training here received as members of The Boys' Brigade when engaged in the great 'Fight for Right' on the battlefront.*

Orphan Homes of Scotland, Bridge of Weir. The Band in Pre. B.B. Days

The annual inspection of 1912 revealed a thriving Coy. who in addition to their drill & physical exercises attended classes for First Aid, Vocal Music, Gymnastics (The school had been given a new set of apparatus for the school hall in 1911) and Swimming. The Company were complimented on their 'Smart appearance' by the Brigade Secretary Sir William A Smith.

In 1911 the Chairman of the School managers had been a certain 'J.P. Maclay' a local benefactor. By 1918 he had become Sir Joseph Maclay. Presiding over the re-formed Company's (now called '1st' Bridge of Weir) first Display on May 2nd 1933 LORD Maclay was impressed with the efficiency of the Boys who had less than thirty parades behind them. The Company was still strong in June 1936 when Lord Rowallan (Elected Chief Scout in February 1945) was Inspecting Officer.

In 1947 Sir Joseph (Later Lord) Maclay (The son of Lord Maclay, described above) Inspected the Coy's Life Boys and also became National Boys' Brigade President taking over from Lord Home; a position he held until 1963. At the Annual Church Parade of Quarrier's homes Uniformed organizations in May 1948 he read the scripture Lesson in Church and took the salute at the close of the service. The Maclays, local landowners, were always associated with the Quarrier's Homes. Lord Maclay today holds the honour of being Lord Chancellor.

2nd Bridge of Weir Coy. c1912

[Reproduced with the kind permission of the Brigade Secretary of The Boys Brigade.]

2nd Bridge of Weir Coy. c1911

8TH BIRMINGHAM COMPANY   THE BOYS' BRIGADE

If only each Company photograph could tell its own story, its history, the stories of its characters old & young; members for a short time or those who have 'come through the ranks'. Boys, N.C.O.'s, Officers, Chaplains. Perhaps much would be revealed that has been lost in the mists of time. Fine, old, large companies peopled by 'Individuals' who thrived upon the electrical energy of 'esprit-de-corps', charged their batteries and went out into the world as beacons . . passing on their discovery like an olympic torch to those who would follow . . those who would carry on. It's not all idle sentiment.

Such a story emerges from the pictures of the 8th Birmingham Coy shown here in 1912/13 & c1930 outside their Church; Islington Methodist St Martin's Street. The pictures cannot talk, but some of the people on them can, along with their deeds and actions over best part of a Century.

8th B'ham. B.B. 1912/13

The eighth was founded in 1906 by D. Gordon Barnsley the son of Sir John Barnsley who was at the time President of the 1st B'ham Coy. That's Gordon Barnsley in the centre of the 1912/13 photo, next to the minister Rev Beecham. Large as it evidently was in those days, the company often paraded at Gordon Barnsley's house for an Inspection, he was a leader who inspired both fellow officers and Boys.

On the 1912/13 photograph on the other side of the Rev Beecham stands a young 2nd Lt by the name of Sweyn Barnes. 'S.E. Barnes' was a young officer greatly infused with the spirit of the B.B. but the 1st World War interrupted his B.B. Career as well as equipping him for later life. He was sent to Australia in 1915 as an army training Officer. The 8th Coy at the same time suffered the fate of many, in having to close down for the duration of the conflict. Gordon Barnsley took over the 3rd Coy based at the Central Hall. When the war was over and Sweyn Barnes returned to the 8th, he was able to take over as Captain.

'S.E.' made a first class job as Captain as can be witnessed in the photograph of a very smart Coy under his command c1930. He was to leave Birmingham again but this time in the Service of the B.B. in 1938 to take up an appointment as the first B.B. H.Q. Secretary for training, a position which enabled him to become a National figure in the B.B. for which he was awarded the O.B.E. for his services in 1958. It was 'S.E.' who was responsible for finding and equipping Felden Lodge the Brigade's National training Centre in Hertfordshire; still used today for the same purpose. A recently departed lifelong friend of S.E.B. and sadly missed B'ham B.B. Capt (Former Hon. Batt President and Brigade Vice-President) Harold Burnett M.B.E. writing Sweyn Barnes's obituary in 1976 described him as a 'stickler' for tradition' but always friendly and approachable.

Back to the 1912/13 photo . . and the twins, with crossed haversacks in the second row near the centre. Albert (L) and George (R) Oakton had been in the Brigade for just two sessions; the crossed haversacks were only worn by recipients of the Ambulance Badge, proudly displayed by the Boys. The twins really enjoyed their time in the Company, taking part not only in ambulance classes but football, swimming, Sailor's Drill and even using cutlasses on one occasion.

Camp 1913 at Weston-Super-Mare was the highlight of that year for the twins. 'I saw the sea for the first time' said George. When William Smith came to the Central Hall B'ham as the chief guest at the annual Battalion Display the boys felt honoured as they looked up eagerly at the great man; they had won the Drill shield in 1911 the previous year... wouldn't it be ripping to win it here in front of Smith? Unfortunately it was not to be their year, but the great man took the time to shake them by the hand.

The Company   c1930

Both George & Albert stayed on to become Officers in the 8th supporting S.E. Barnes. Albert eventually left the Coy when his job with the Hospitals took him away to Worthing. What a good foundation the ambulance class must have been for Albert, for in 1964 Albert Victor Oakton Esq., F.H.A. retired as group secretary of the Worthing Group Hospitals management Committee. George was only around as an Officer in the 8th for a short time when, in 1922 he was asked to help out with the 5th B'ham Coy who were short staffed. Twelve months later saw George as Captain Oakton of the 5th working hard to build up the Company under great difficulties of finance and accommodation. The Brigade spirit was to win through however, in the 1930's the 5th's numbers began to increase and George Oakton instituted as many activities as possible particularly First-Aid. (In the Mid 1970's Bernard Thomas the famous MCC 'Physio' who helped to save the life of N.Z. Cricketer Ewan Chatfield had put to use valuable lessons learnt as a Boy in the 5th under George Oakton).

During the Second World War the 5th Coy manned the First Aid post at Kent Street under the direction of Capt. Oakton. In a severe bombing raid one night, Kent St suffered a direct hit with the F.A.P. being destroyed. Two Boys were seriously injured and one, sadly, died. George continued his war work and was awarded the B.E.M. for his efforts.

George W. Oakton B.E.M. has served the BB in Birmingham continuously since 1911, for many years as Hon. Vice President. In the last few years cutting down on the number of events attended but still 'turning out' when required at an age (as I write) of 91 years!

Many Brigade companies have similar stories, only a few have been told. The contribution of the Brigades to our National life begins to take on greater meaning when seen amidst the tumult of an age of change and conflict in Europe. The importance of a firm foundation steering youth to better things becomes self-evident.

1ST ENFIELD COY. BOYS BRIGADE.

[Reproduced with the kind permission of the Brigade Secretary of The Boys Brigade]

Tea in Capt. Ridge's Garden 1916.

Capt. R. Leslie Ridge of 1st Enfield Coy was the son of the Coy's founder, prominent local non-conformist and Medical Officer of health Dr. J.J. Ridge (1847-1908). In 1888 'J.J.' had been impressed by reading about the success of William Smith's Brigade, since he too was running a Sunday School. Dr Ridge's son was, no doubt, continuing a tradition established by his father when he invited the N.C.O.'s round for tea. By 1916 he had already taken over the Captaincy of the Coy and the Medical Practice from his father. In this picture Mrs Ridge is one of the ladies standing, with his daughter in the centre. Originally, most of the Boys of the 1st worked in the new Edison & Swan Light Bulb factory in nearby Ponders End. The present members of 1st Enfield Coy (Lancaster Rd Congregational Church) celebrated their hundredth birthday in 1988. Dr Ridge wrote the B.B. 'Ambulance Handbook' in 1939, a publication which sold over 140,000 copies.

Indian Clubs Kaleidoscope 1st Enfield Coy. B.B. 1945

This picture postcard was written on October 4th 1945 complete with 'Best wishes' to celebrate 'Founding Day'; the day the Boys' Brigade was founded in 1883. The 1st Enfield, still under their 'Skipper' Dr R. Leslie Ridge were obviously a large & successful Company. The Card was written from 'Carleton House', Enfield the home and surgery of the Ridges until it was demolished a few years ago to make way for an Old Persons' Home. Dr. Ridge writes. . 'My Dear Roy. .' to an N.C.O. who had 'signed on' again for the new session. Dr Ridge states that in his case he will make allowances for homework; perhaps he was getting mellow in his old age? In 1910 he had dismissed 19 members of the Coy due to 'lack of loyalty' after which girlfriends were banned from all Coy activities. He was a believer in discipline.

Unfortunately, some of Dr Ridge's writing on the back of the card is illegible . . but he was a doctor after all!

ROGER S. PEACOCK & THE 76TH LONDON COY. B.B.

THE BOYS' BRIGADE, 76TH LONDON COMPANY.

Private J. Walker of Catford, a member of the 76th London Coy received these two cards within days of each other on Dec 28th 1906 and Jan 2nd 1907. They were sent by the Coy. Capt. They illustrate very well the early 'undivided back' type card still popular years after divided backs were commonplace. The Captain is using the cards as a quick way of contacting his Company. Who today would consider using the post to let someone know that there would be 'no football match tomorrow' or to request help in organising 'tomorrow's supper'?

This personal attention to the members of his Company however comes from the pencil & pen of Roger Stephen Peacock, a man who gave a lifetime's service to the B.B.

As a young Officer in 1902 Roger Peacock became the first London District secretary at the B.B. H.Q. in Paternoster Row. Before retiring from the Brigade in 1947 he had served under William Smith and his son Stanley Smith occupying various Brigade positions. He originated the idea of BB 'Rest Huts' for soldiers in the 1914/18 war and was the chief architect of many B.B. Institutions such as the Royal Albert Hall display and 'BB Week'. He wrote hymns, articles and prayers as well as the book 'Pioneer of Boyhood' the Biography of W.A. Smith.

He stayed with his beloved 76th London Coy throughout the worst bombing of the second world war. Captain for nearly 40 years the Coy. was described as the 'Jewel of his heart'.

Many Boys (The author included!) will have happy memories of camping at Whitecliff Bay, Isle of Wight where Peacock pioneered BB Camping at the top of what has become officially known as 'Peacock Hill'.

Roger Stephen Peacock died on 11th November 1965 aged 88 yrs.

BOYS' OWN BRIGADE

___7___ COMPANY, [Mill St.]

WEEKLY ORDERS

Week ending _Decr. 14_ 19 11.

Display, 14th Decr.

The Company will fall in at 7.30 pm with drummers and buglers.

Members are reminded that particular attention must be shown to cleanness and smartness of uniforms; boots must be well polished, and clothing neat and clean.

Practice 13th Decr.

The company will fall in at 7.0 pm for a final preparatory practice. Buglers and drummers will attend.

Examination (November)

The following, having obtained the requisite percentage of marks in the recent examination have qualified for the rank of Lance-Corporal—

Pte Richd. Rosser   Pte Robert Randles
" Hy. Rimmer (Band)   " Chas Liggett
" C. Jones

The following, who passed in March last, have again passed

LCpl. John Rosser   Pte. Hough
" J. Whewell   " G. McMechane.
" T. Salisbury
" Radcliffe.

Signed _HWBarr_
Captain.

4. WE DID IT OUR WAY

Variety, they say, is the 'spice of life'. If we continue the analogy further then the first thirty years of the century produced the most pungent and piquant mixture of 'Brigade' organizations.

The 'major' Brigades have already been introduced, they thrived at a time when sectarianism was considered a virtuous course to follow. There were those who could not resist 'doing their own thing' within the limits of a parent organisation. Others simply formed their own 'Brigade' to suit their Town, Village, Coalmine, Religious Sect etc.

No forage caps or field-service hats for most of these B.B. Boys! In the early part of the century many rather unorthodox variants of uniform developed along with, in some cases, unorthodox organizations. 'Slouch Hats' like these were approved for Camp wear by a number of the Brigades, but with regular uniform…and feathers? William Smith would not have been amused.

Where Did You Get That Hat? Hull Battalion B.B. Camp Mappleton 1910
This Photograph by Overton's of Hull & Hornsea shows the bewildering variety of attire. In some cases resembling uniform but for the most part a cross between 'mufti" & 'Undress' The young man in the foreground is wearing a sailor-suit the 'de rigueur' of the period for young Boys. Another version of 'doing your own thing'… how many hat styles can you spot?

THE BOYS' OWN BRIGADE

In the closing decade of the nineteenth century, religious intolerance had developed almost as quickly as the many new sects and groups within the Non-Conformist Protestant Churches. 'Catholicity' was frowned upon by many, particularly that variety expounded by the Unitarian Church.

It all started with the 46th London Coy. The Boys' Brigade, based at the amalgamated Blackfriars Mission Lambeth and Stamford St. Chapels. As the Company started to participate in Battalion activities within the South London Battalion, the Boys' Brigade Executive realised that they were *'In close touch with Unitarian thought and teaching'* The South London B.B. had not objected but a few members of the B.B. Executive were resentful and after much correspondence caused the Company to cease in June 1899. Relationships with the B.B. however, remained amicable; so much so that Secretary William Smith encouraged the officers to continue with a 'Brigade', making all B.B. literature available to them.

The Staff of the 'dissolved' Company, who had left the Brigade *'With much regret'* were far from dis-heartened, in fact they were keen to continue with the Brigade Method. With their Minister they began to formulate ideas for their own 'Brigade'. Suggestions were made by Smith for it to be called 'Unitarian Boys' Brigade'... but in the true liberal spirit of their Church they felt that membership should not be seen as restricted to those holding any special theological views.

In October 1899 the new Brigade was instituted with the old '46th' becoming the No. 1. Coy of the 'Boys Own Brigade'. The significance of the 'Own' being that the Brigade was *'For the full rounded development of the Boys themselves, and not for the spread of theological dogma, military spirit or any branch of social reform.'*

Rev. John C. Ballantyne; Founder, Hon. Sec., Treasurer and Captain of No. 1. Coy launched the Brigade virtually single-handed, struggling along for the first few years to develop the organization. It was June 1909 before the 'First Annual Report' could be issued detailing the constitution and 'progress' of the B.O.B. Ballantyne admitted in the report that development had not been rapid, due to lack of workers and the 'fear of militarism'. Expansion to four companies in London had reduced down to two at one time. However by 1909 they were back to five Companies in the London Battalion and considerable progress was taking place.

In the early years Miss Marian Pritchard had helped the B.O.B. considerably (She wrote extensively under the pseudonym 'Aunt Amy' in young peoples magazines). Her death in 1908 was a considerable setback to the Brigade.

THE BOYS' OWN BRIGADE MOVEMENT.

(1) and (2) Members Liverpool Company, Capt. McCann, Mill-street Mission ; (3) Officers and Cooks, Liverpool Camp, 1912 ; (4) Dutch Camp Group, from the Volkshuis, Leiden, managed by W. E. van Wijk, who learned his camp lessons with the B.O.B.: (5) Rev. J. C. Ballantyne ; (6) and (7) Liverpool Camp, 1912 ; (8) Mr. Ronald P. Jones.

[Extract from 'Christian Life' May 1913. E. Basil Short]

Mr. Ion Pritchard (Marian's brother) was appointed the first president of the B.O.B. with a number of London's leading Unitarians supporting or actively participating in the B.O.B. by 1909.

The Object (In 1909) was:
    'to increase pure and upright living among Boys and to promote habits of helpfulness, obedience, discipline, self-respect, and all that tends towards true manliness.'

The Motto: 'Quit You Like Men – Be Strong!'

Membership was open to Boys aged 12-17 yrs. Staff Sgts from 17-20 yrs. Officers; Gentlemen of 20 yrs upwards.

B.O.B. Uniform was similar to the other Brigades. Cap, Belt & Haversack. The forage cap had two yellow stripes of braid, not white like the B.B. and belt buckles had 'Boys Own Brigade' with a central Logo made up of the initials 'B.O.B.' intertwined in the popular 'Art Nouveau' style which became the B.O.B. Badge; designed and drawn by Mrs Ballantyne. (John had married in 1908).

By 1910 the B.O.B. had spread to Liverpool with two new Companies formed. Attempts at starting others in Bolton, Manchester, Sheffield & Leigh were not so successful. However, by 1913 the number of Companies had risen to eleven with Coy's numbered up to 12. John Ballantyne moved to Nottingham. Mr Ronald P. Jones MA became President; he was an Architect and brother of C. Sydney Jones Director of the Blue Funnel shipping Line.

The Object was changed, by 1913, to read: *'to promote habits of helpfulness, discipline, self-respect and reverence, and to quicken and sustain among its members a spirit of comradeship and of consecration to the service of God. This object shall be advanced by means of drill (not associated with the use of arms), gymnastic practice, instruction in first-aid, life-saving, musical instruction, religious services etc.'*

49

In the B.O.B. they had their own Hymns: 'Lend a Hand' & 'Reveille' and published their own Hymn Book 'The Boys Own Book of Hymns & Songs'. Other activities included Annual Camp, the London Battalion at Walnut Tree Farm, Deal, Kent... in the field next to the giant J.L.B. Camp and near a L.D.C.L.B. Camp. Good relationships were developed with both Brigades, although comments were made about the L.D.C.L.B.'s use of Rifles for Drill. The B.O.B. were the only Brigade asked to join the National Council of Peace Organizations (In 1910)... Ballantyne had written: *'We carried no rifles . . not even broomsticks'* this was to keep the B.O.B. free from the 'taint' of militarism. Liverpool Battalion camped together, often on the Isle of Man, developing good relationships with the West Lancs B.L.B.

THE COMPANIES OF THE BOYS' OWN BRIGADE

		Formed
No. 1.	Stamford St Chapel/Blackfriars Mission, London.	1899
No. 2.	Rhyl St. Mission. Kentish Town, London	
No. 3.	Mansford St. Church & Mission. Bethnal Green, London.	
No. 4.	Essex Church. Notting Hill Gate, London.	1908
No. 5.	George's Row Mission. Clerkenwell, London.	1908
No. 6.	Bell St. Mission, London.	
No. 7.	Liverpool Domestic Mission. Mill St.	
No. 8.	Hamilton Rd. Domestic Mission. Liverpool.	1910
No. 9.	Birkenhead. Liverpool.	1912
No. 10.	Monton ?	
No. 11.	Bootle	
No. 12.	New Gravel Pit Church, Hackney, London.	1913

Like all Brigades, the 1914-18 war took its toll from the B.O.B. with 120 members and ex-members serving in the army in 1915. The B.O.B. survived the war and John Ballantyne moved to the Liverpool Domestic Mission at Mill St, home of the B.O.B. No. 7 Coy., where he was to stay until 1935. Mr Barker was B.O.B. Capt. of No 7 at the time. By 1920 the B.O.B. were back at Camp on Walnut Tree Farm. Adjutant, Lt George Holmes, one of the original B.O.B. Boys from No 3 Coy at Mansford St. with war service in France behind him, was well equipped to provide an efficient Camp.

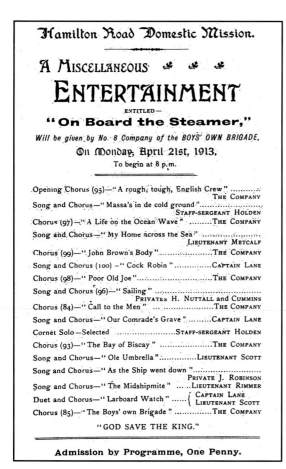

[Liverpool Record Office]

It is from Liverpool however, that we can trace the gradual demise of the B.O.B. Around 1925 Mr G.D. Foot a lay assistant to Rev Ballantyne, persuaded him to introduce 'Scouting'. The B.O.B. members had their 'Boys Own Club' and an 'Old Boys Fellowship' which gradually absorbed the B.O.B. When Ballantyne left Mill St in 1935 to return to London (Essex St) there was no No 4 B.O.B. Coy still operating, it too had been absorbed into a Boys' Club; so he tried to introduce scouting there, without much success. A Company of 'The Boys' Brigade' was operating at Essex St in 1951 but had gone by the time John Ballantyne left in 1957. Ballantyne retired to Christchurch, Dorset in 1958 and died c 1963.

In 1913 a 'GIRLS OWN BRIGADE' was formed at the New Gravel Pit Church in Hackney. By 1915 there were three Coys: No 1 Hackney, No 2 Ilford, & No 3 Brixton. Miss E.H. Green was the Hon. sec. The Girls had a 'costume' of navy blue blouses and skirt with crimson collar, cuffs, tie and belt. The Badge depicted the 'Brigade Flower' the daisy, which *Loves the sunshine and is always looking up* The motto: 'Tender, Trusty and True' (From one of Dr Collyer's sermons). The Brigade Promise: 'I promise to be Tender, Trusty & True and to keep the rules of the Brigade and to make a bit of sunshine for someone every day.' Activities included making their costumes, drill with bars, flags, balls and dumb-bells, Unison Singing, home nursing, story-telling and games.

Chipping Norton Boys' Own Brigade Camp at Curdle Hill August 1908
A Picture Postcard from Chipping Norton's famous publisher Frank Packer. This group were not an official part of the B.O.B.... they may have 'used' their name or taken it from the 'Boys Own Paper', which had as its staple; like other penny magazines of the day, daring adventure stories from around the Empire. Boys were keen to experience for themselves the 'Manly Christianity' of their heroes.

All over Britain there were small Brigades developing; at least two versions of the 'Gordon Boys' Brigade' (Liverpool & Southsea), Boys Rifle Brigade (Leeds), Boys Ambulance Brigade, Lads' Drill Association (formed by Lord Meath), Boys Life Guards (Rev T.A. Leonard), Imperial Lads' Brigade (West Hartlepool). Individual Churches sometimes sponsored their own 'Brigades'... St Mary's B.B. etc.

BOYS' OWN BRIGADE,

COMPANY No. 7. *Liverpool.*

OFFICERS' REPORT.

Week ending 2nd April 1914

Signalling :-

The following boys have satisfied the Examiners and have been awarded badges by the Battalion Executive :-

Semaphore Code :
L/c. Christian
Pte H. Taft
" A. Baylis
" R. Coates
} Average time 52 letters in 2 minutes.

Morse Code :
Pte J. Williams
" Wm. Harrison
} average time 49 letters in 2 minutes.

Certificate signed by J.P. Forwood Heyn
Scoutmaster 27th L'pool Troop Scouts.

Promotion :-

The Captain is pleased to approve the following appointment :-
Pte J. Williams to be Corporal Signaller
Signed .... H. Hall ....
(Captain)

Domestic Mission, Mill Street.

THE BOYS' OWN BRIGADE

(7th Company, Liverpool),

WILL GIVE THEIR

Annual Display,

On Tuesday, 7th April, 1914,

Commencing at 8 p.m.

—— Programme. ——

1. COMPANY DRILL.
2. SELECTIONS BY THE BAND.
3. DISPLAY BY JUNIOR CORPS.
4. FIRST AID DISPLAY.
5. GYMNASTIC DISPLAY.
6. { SIGNALLING (Morse and Semaphore).
   { LIFE SAVING.
7. To conclude with a Short Entertainment by the BOYS' OWN MINSTRELS.

' GOD SAVE THE KING."

ADMISSION BY PROGRAMME, 2d.

[Liverpool Record Office]

THE NEW CHURCH BOYS' BRIGADE

The N.C.B.B. was one of the so-called, 'Secretarian' Brigades formed in the closing decade of the 19th Century when enthusiasm for the new Brigade movement had reached its zenith.

The New Church did not approve then, as they would not today, of the title 'sectarian' for their Church or Brigade. The religious books of Emanuel Swedenborg written some two hundred years ago, form the basis for the teaching of the Church, which differs from many 'sectarian' Christian Non-Conformist churches in that it shuns dogma for the religion of life.

Like most Sunday Schools at the time, those of the New Church were strong in numbers, with a well organised Junior Members Society and Young People's Guild; however, some of the leaders saw the 'Brigade Method' as a useful supplement to the work. In some areas the N.C.B.B. suffered critics in the community because of being part of the New Church, and more critics within the New Church Societies because of alleged 'militarism'.

The strength of the New Church lay in the Cotton towns of Lancashire and it was in Kearsley, Manchester that the first Company was founded by Rev. G. Beswick Meek B.A. in October 1896. Influential members of the New Church Sunday School Union, in particular Mr. J. Stuart Bogg, threw their weight behind the Brigade to help its launch and development. Stuart Bogg becoming its first 'Colonel' and later President.

By B.B. or C.L.B. standards the development of the N.C.B.B. was not rapid, perhaps due to an insistence upon attendance at Sunday School, opposition within the church and the limited number of New Church Societies. The situation was not helped when Mr Meek, Brigade Adjutant and Secretary went to America for most of 1903, Asst. Adjutant Penton removed to London and Col. Bogg was incapacitated, recovering from an accident, for twelve months. By 1900 four Companies had been started and by 1903 this number had risen to Seven fully active (with a total of about 203 Boys) including only one outside Lancashire.

Draft Constitutions (based upon those of the C.L.B. & B.L.B.) were published from 1900-1903, with final acceptance in late 1903. The object was:

'... to train Boys connected with New Church Sunday Schools in habits of discipline, order and self-control, also in active Church Work of suitable kinds, – that they may become citizens in the Lord's Kingdom.'

The ages were specified as 10-17 yrs for Boys on the roll of a New Church Sunday School.

Boys' Uniform was ratified in the constitution as; Scarlet and White Forage Cap, Brown Leather waist Belt, White Haversack, with optional Water Bottle. The distinctive Swastika Emblem with the motto 'Onward & Upward' also came into being in 1903 appearing on metal Badges awarded for regular attendance and worn on the Cap, as well as featuring on the Flag. N.C.B.B. flags were Red and White with a large Blue Swastika 'cross'. The Red & White were said to signify the 'Infinite wisdom and Love of the Lord, equal and indivisible'. The Swastika emblem is an ancient symbol of 'well being' from the East, found in the sanskrit language. It would have been interesting to note the comments of the locals in say, South Essex, in the Late 1930's (had it been possible) watching a parade of uniformed Boys marching down their High Street behind a large Swastika Flag, which by then had taken on a wholly more sinister meaning!

It is unlikely however, that the N.C.B.B. survived the trauma of the 1st World war. Growth had been erratic at the best of times and in 1911 it was reported in the Church's 'Morning Light' magazine '... it is a regrettable fact that the number of companies of the N.C.B.B. is steadily diminishing.'

Activities of the N.C.B.B. were very similar to most Brigades of the time. They described themselves as mainly a 'Life-Saving Brigade' with much stress being placed on First Aid and Ambulance work along with swimming and Life Saving training. A Camp of 140 N.C.B.B. Boys under the command of Mr Beswick Meek was

'H' Company New Church Boys' Brigade, Brightlingsea c1909.

[Neville Gray]

organised in 1901 at Rivington Pike from August 3rd-6th but a commentator writing in 'Morning Light' under the pseudonym 'Eye Witness' was not impressed: *'I feel constrained to confess that one or two of the Companies require and will have to learn, a little more discipline and obedience. The same may also be said of one or two of the Officers'* Generally behaviour of N.C.B.B. Boys was praised in New Church Publications. The 1903 Constitution indicated that perhaps there had been a problem with 'model Rifles' (pictures before this time show rifles being carried), it stated: *'any Company possessing sham guns shall employ them solely for the purpose of Physical Exercises'* It can be imagined what criticism was faced by some of the Officers; one or two Church members wanted to see the Brigade return to its 'original function' of 'Tract Distribution'.

Music played an important role in the N.C.B.B. Fife Bands were gradually replaced by Bugle Bands, a special march called the 'New Church Call' was written in 1903. The Brigade Hymn composed by J. Stuart Bogg was 'Awake! Awake! Ye sons of light' with a special Hymn being written called 'Boys of the New Church Brigade'.

Perhaps the most remarkable aspect of the N.C.B.B. was the participation of females! In 1901 the Salford Company had two lady Officers. In October 1903 a 'Girls Auxiliary Brigade' was formed at Salford with a No 2 Company at N. Manchester (Broughton) and No 3 at Ashton-U-Lyne. Other Companies notably at Argyle Square London were also formed later. 'Girls Brigade' members were often to be found participating in N.C.B.B. events including 'March-outs' and Church Parades.

Reports of co-operation and fratemization with other Brigades are remarkably common. Brightlingsea Essex, was the destination each Summer for a Number of Companies of The Boys' Brigade from Ipswich, Stowmarket & Brentford for their annual Camp including a detachment of C.L.B. In 1903 the visiting Brigades were met at the station by the 1st Brightlingsea B.B., Brightlingsea C.L.B. and 'H' Coy. New Church Boys' Brigade who then paraded with them into camp with colours flying and Bands playing. Later in the week they all marched to St Osyth's for a day out in the park at the priory, five bands were playing on the march. An observer reported that the 'H' Coy N.C.B.B. were the 'prettiest' with their Red & White hats, the C.L.B. came second with their Blue & Gold.

OFFICERS AND BOYS OF "K" COMPANY, NORTH MANCHESTER, 1903.

[The New Church Society]

List of Known New Church B.B. Companies with Dates of Foundation

'A'	Kearsley	Oct.	1896	
'B'	Salford	By	1900	
'C'	Preston	By	1900	
'D'	Liverpool	By	1900	
'E'	Heywood		1901	(Re-Formed 1906)
'F'	Wigan		1901	
'F'	Worsley		1904	
'G'	London		1901	
'G'	South Manchester		1903	
'H'	Brightlingsea	June	1902	
'H'	London (Argyle Sq)		1903	
'H'	Brightlingsea		1909	
'I'	Salford		1901	
'I'	Pendleton		1902	
'K'	Manchester (N)		1902	(Re-formed)*
'K'	Radcliffe		1907	
'K'	Brightlingsea		1909	
'N'	Ashton U Lyne	Aug.	1903	

*Originally formed (In 1901) as Coy of 'Boys Ambulance Brigade'

In April 1908 a Company was formed in Nottingham but there is no record of the allocated letter.

References to the N.C.B.B. in New Church publications diminish rapidly after 1911 with increasing references to the formation of Boy Scout Troops.

THE BOLTON BOYS' BRIGADE [1908-1960]

The Bolton Battalion of The Boys' Brigade started in 1887 when the 1st Coy was established at Victoria Wesley Church in Grecian Crescent. The development of the Brigade in the Town followed along similar lines to the rest of Britain except for the fact that many of the Officers were from a military background and did not, consequently, wholly agree with the lack of hierarchy... indeed blatant equality displayed by the B.B. Staff. Not for them, Smith's idea of only one Officer rank! A few concessions were made; in 1895 a resolution was passed at the Battalion Council meeting that: *'the wearing of swords be discarded'.*

By 1906, it had become clear that the Battalion were out of step with the rest of the Brigade; alternative uniform proposals had been rejected and William Smith was unable to persuade them to toe the line. By a small majority, the whole Battalion voted to leave the Brigade in 1906.

'The Bolton Boys' Brigade' as they now were, had the freedom to change things as they wished... and they did. The Anchor emblem was replaced by the town's Elephant & Castle coat of arms, used on belt buckles, badges and letterheads along with the latin inscription 'Semper Paratus' [Always Ready] replacing 'Sure & Stedfast'. Until 1922 the Object of the Brigade remained almost the same as the B.B. with the words *'Advancement of Christ's Kingdom'* omitted. By 1931 a new Object had appeared:

'...to give moral and physical training to Boys, to enable them to make a good start in life; to develop in them principles of patriotism and good citizenship, and to form a link between the Boys in the Brigade and the church with which the Company is connected.'

New awards were needed for the new Brigade and they were provided in only a moderate number; a Three year service badge. Efficiency Badge, Long Service medal, (5 yrs) with bars for additional periods of five years. (Officers only). Drummers, Buglers & Ambulance awards were also used.

Between 1907 and 1908 numbers declined in the B.B.B. casting doubt upon the wisdom of the break with the B.B.

A Junior Organization called the 'Bantam Boys' was instituted for Boys aged 8 – 10 yrs with a uniform consisting of School Cap (With inverted 'V' white piping and Company number worn at the front. A horizontally striped blue & white tie was also worn with the option of a blue jersey with buttons at the top, or 'normal clothing'.

Boys' uniform all through the New Brigade had to be changed. Besides belts with the Elephant Emblem a Forage Cap with a decorative braid on the crown was used. Staff Sgts had peaked caps with three stripes not two. Faced with supply problems from 1940 onwards the 'pill box' cap was replaced by berets and field service caps.

When Boys became members of The Bolton B.B. they were known as 'Cadets'; the whole Brigade being run as one large unit broken down into Companies. It became a 'centrally controlled' organization, for instance 'Camp' meant 'Brigade Camp' individual Companies were not allowed to Camp on their own. Company numbers were often 'switched around' to suit the Brigade who operated a whole Staff... needless to say each with his own rank: Hon. Colonel was Lt Col. W.E. Walker.

At its peak there were only thirteen Coys in the B.B.B., some of them existing as 'Band' companies. Bands were very important in the Brigade as a Report of the 1914 Annual Brigade Church Parade shows... when it describes a 29 member Military Band with commanding Officer on horseback along with two other mounted Officers behind. Six Hundred Cadets, 11 Bands including Bugle/Drum, Trumpets, Pipes, Fifes, and Bersac Cor (Keyed Bugle).

In 1909 Bolton B.B. 'Scouts' were officially recognised, mirroring the development of Scouting in the Boys' Brigades nationally.

No. 1 Co. Bolton B.B. 1925 Camp Abergele (353 Boys at Camp)
Captain: Norman Walker & Instructor Billy Wood. Note the decorative crown on the forage caps and the Captain's uniform.

Although affiliated to the Government's Cadet Scheme for many years, it was 11th Feb 1921 before the B.B.B. became officially recognised as a 'Cadet Battalion' taking advantage of 4-5 shillings per Cadet given as a grant for P.E. Equipment and Camping facilities. The B.B.B. remained in the Cadet scheme until its closure in 1930, a full six years after its 'parent' B.B. had left. The B.B.B. had been members of the East Lancs Territorial Assoc. As soon as the 'British National Cadet Assoc.' was formed the B.B.B. continued its membership for as long as possible.

Good relationships existed with the B.B. throughout the period of 'Independence' mainly due to the auspices of Normal Leigh Hon. Sec. from 1905 – 1960. Norman had known William Smith and continued to respect him as the man responsible for the B.B. in Bolton. In 1960 the B.B.B. re-united with The Boys' Brigade.

[Reproduced with the kind permission of the Brigade Secretary of The Boys Brigade]

No. 1 Co. Bolton B.B. c1950 Camp. Bridlington [196 Boys at Camp]
Captain: A.J. Tatlock is pictured in centre with his dog 'Peggy'. Capt Tatlock Battalion Secretary 1960 to 1970, was one of the Officers who helped steer the B.B.B. back into happy union with the rest of the B.B. Note the variety of headgear worn at this time; Berets, Field Srevice Caps & Sgts. Peaked caps.

Looking after the injured. The 'Ambulance' squad from No. 6 Co. at Rhyl Camp 1913. No doubt they were kept busy, with 446 members at Camp that year.

He who cannot obey will never be fit to rule.

Don't wait until you're a man to be great, BE A GREAT BOY.

Keep Smiling.

Be A Sport.

FIRST CADET BATTALION
BOLTON BOYS' BRIGADE
NO. 14 COMPANY.

Wesley Church, Castle Street, Bolton.

Teach me to win when I may, and, if I may not win, then above all, make me a good loser.

'Anyone entering our tent will be bashed'
Four Boys from No 10 Co. at Camp, determined to create injury!

Cards given out to Boys by Capt. Lomax. No. 14. Co. B.B.B.

Members of the No. 14 Co. Bolton B.B. on parade in Capt. Lomax's Garden (Late 1930's)

[Dave Thomas]

A Young Cadet from No 14 Co. Bolton B.B. c1915

[Stephen Hulcoop]

No 14 Co. Bolton B.B. Church Parade c1956.

[Dave Thomas]

No 14 Co were based at the Castle St. Methodist Church and were formed in 1914 when the Church opened. The Co. Captain was Mr. John S. Lomax, a member of the Joshua Barber Cotton Waste Merchants family.

Happy faces at a B.B.B. Bible Class. (1950's)

[Dave Thomas]

A Newspaper article once described the B.B.B. as being:

'mainly Methodist and run by the sons of wealthy mill owners with nothing else to spend their money on'

THE BOLSOVER COLLIERY CO. BOYS BRIGADE

Just as each religious group in Britain at the turn of the century wanted its share in the blossoming Boys' Brigade movement, so it was with some philanthropic industrial concerns with their truly socialistic creed of 'cradle to grave' models of society fired by religious conviction and dreams of utopia. Such concern was rightly, regarded as far-sighted in a world where worker exploitation, apalling living conditions, drunkeness and non-existent recreation facilities were very much the 'norm'. A classic example of this genre of 'caring capitalism' was the Bolsover Colliery Company, N. Nottinghamshire.

Founded in 1889, the Company developed a total of six coal mines in its 58 year history. Adjacent to each mine was built a 'model village'; cottages with five rooms, gardens, yards, wide streets, playgrounds, clubs institutes, drill halls and sports grounds. Naturally, with all the physical pre-requisites of social organization there developed, sponsored by 'the Company' of course, Boys Brigade Companies, Girls Brigade Companies, Ambulance Brigades, Brass Bands and all manner of groups vowed to increase the physical, social and moral well-being of the community and the Nation.

The Bolsover Colliery Co's Mines & Dates of Development:

Bolsover	1891	
Creswell	1896	
Mansfield	1905	(Forest Town Village)
Rufford	1911	(Rainworth Village)
Clipstone	1922	
Thoresby	1928	(Edwinstowe)

Cresswell Colliery B.B. 1909
The Second Company of the Bolsover Colliery B.B., by 1909 they were 140 strong. On parade here are the Brass Band, the junior Brigade members (With 'Pill Box' hats) and the Senior members in full uniform. Note the Officers uniform and the cottages of the 'model village' in the background.

SIR WILLIAM ROBSON, M.P., AT FOREST TOWN.

BOYS' BRIGADE DRILL HALL OPENED.

ATTORNEY GENERAL ON NATIONAL DEFENCE.

DRILL HALL, FOREST TOWN.

A report in the Mansfield & N. Notts Advertiser on 21st May 1909 on the opening of the Boys' Brigade Drill Hall at Forest Town by Sir William Robson K.G. M.P. (Attorney General) reveals much about the socio-political climate of the time. A large crowd gathered for the opening, a guard of honour being formed by the 130 strong Mansfield Boys' Brigade, for whom the hall was intended, along with 140 from the Creswell Brigade. The Hall, it was announced, had been built by The Bolsover Colliery Company *'For recreation and social enjoyment of the younger members of the community associated with Mansfield colliery'* It was fitted with Gym apparatus, reading room, billiards room and others. There was a speech from Mr Emerson Bainbridge thanking the Landlord the Duke of Portland for being a major subscriber to the Hall. Three Colliery villages had been built, it was stated, for the 6,000 workers who due to the fine social conditions had lost little work through drunkeness or illness. The Hall was declared to be *'the finest Boys' Brigade Drill Hall in the Kingdom'*.

Not wishing to confine himself, as a member of H.M. Government, to Forest Town alone, Sir William spoke at length about *'Drill in the History of the World'* and inevitably, National Defence. He considered the Boys' Brigade to be the start of the citizen's part in the Nation's defence: *'every class of the community should consider how far it can contribute something to National Defence... those who have joined the Brigade can be told from amongst others in the pit by their superior demeanour and by their smartness of style'*.

Although 'superior demeanour & smartness' could not be detected easily down the pit, the members of the Colliery B.B. certainly had these attributes when above ground. Boys aged under 14 yrs had typical B.B. uniform accoutrements; forage cap with white braid and crown & anchor badge of the Colliery B.B. on the front, (The Crown part of the emblem was that of the Bolsover C.C.), white haversack and leather waistbelt. By the 1920's some Companies had adopted the field-service cap for these younger Boys. Older members had a smart blue full uniform with a service pattern hat; B.C.B.B. Badges on hat and collar. Field-Service hats were used by older members with their full uniforms in Companies which retained forage caps for younger members. Officers had a full uniform with a service pattern hat with one or two changes in style over the years.

A group of senior members of Rufford Colliery B.B. at Rhyl, Aug. 1931. *[Ken Davies]*
Ken Davies is the Drummer (With the drum sling). Note the full uniform with the crown & anchor badges.

Rufford Colliery B.B. In Camp at Skegness 1929

Note the younger Boys with their field-service caps and the older members with 'service' pattern hats. (The full uniform was not yet being worn). Mr Biddulph is the Captain pictured in the centre with other staff messrs: Creswell, Wilson & Wood. The Sgt Major was Jack Phillips. The Drummer far left is Ken Davies along with his colleagues Tommy Jones and Wilf Hinks. Ken, like his friends went to work at the Colliery, for 46 years...even in the 1970's he was running a marching Band in Rainworth village!

Summer Camp was of paramount importance to the colliery Brigade with Skegness, Rhyl, and Bridlington being popular traditional destinations. These Camps were subsidised by the Colliery Company but Boys were still paying 10s per week in the late 1920's! The Brass Bands, one or two nationally known, would often attend camp with the B.B. although there were Brigade Fife Bands and eventually Drum & Bugle Bands.

In 1939, the Colliery Co's Jubilee Year they purchased a permanent Camp for members of the B.B. G.B. and Ambulance Divisions, at Rhyl in N. Wales. This was really a 'Holiday Camp' with permanent buildings in a landscaped setting suitable for 350 persons in addition to the Camp Staff... it wasn't to get much use by the B.B. The six Colliery B.B. Companies had flourished, but the dark clouds of war caused their suspension. In 1947 when the mines were Nationalised the Bolsover Colliery Company ceased to exist along with the fruits of its benevolence; the crown & anchor badge would be seen on B.B. uniforms no more.

Camp Photo: The Bolsover Colliery B.B. c1935 at Bridlington

Note the various types of uniforms as they mass on the railway embankment.

THE CHORLEY BRIGADES

There are no records of either the Boys' Brigade or the Church Lads' Brigade in Chorley Lancs., before 1924. How could this have been, in such a populous area?

The answer to the question above lies, as it so often does, in the hearts, minds and spirit of the people. Lancashire spawned its own Gordon Boys Brigade (Liverpool), its own Diocesan Catholic Boys' Brigade (for a time) at Salford. The Bolton Boys' Brigade and the roots of the New Church Boys' Brigade. The watchword was 'Independence'. Brigade Companies did develop in Chorley, but were not affiliated to the national organizations. They developed instead their own individual style at the various Churches. They were not associated officially and developed great rivalry between each other. They did, however,, follow the basic BB/CLB model copying much of the uniform and activities of their National counterparts.

Typical of these 'Brigades' were the Companies of so-called 'Church Lads' Brigade' at the Anglican Churches of St. James, St Peter and the Parish Church of St Lawrence. Their uniforms were free from all 'C.L.B.' emblems but they did use the Anchor of the Boys' Brigade on their belt buckles (Surrounded by a laurel wreath – A standard pattern from the suppliers catalogue), and later on the front of their service pattern caps. The stated object was similar to that of The Boys Brigade. St Peter's was founded in 1902 and used forage caps initially, changing to Service pattern caps around 1910. St James's Brigade had a distinctive forage cap with a wide white band, before they too changed to 'service' pattern. The Officers had a white crossbelt with a rose emblem and chain.

By the end of March 1924 both St Peter's and St Lawrence's had enrolled in the National C.L.B. St James remaining Independent until 1928. In the 1930's Chorley became a strong C.L.B. Battalion with upwards of 10 Companies under the command of Col. Stroud who was a Headmaster in Adlington. The town still has a Battalion today.

St. Peter's 'C.L.B.' Chorley c1908.
Note: The forage caps without typical C.L.B. Badges & Sgts. Field-Service Caps.

[Stephen Hulcoop]

St. Peter's 'C.L.B. CHORLEY c1910
Note: The 'Service' Pattern hats worn by the Boys. [Nearest to camera]

[Phil Dickinson]

St. James's 'B.B./C.L.B.' (Ref to as both at various times). 1909.
Here seen taking part in the 'Walking Day'. The writer of this picture postcard reports his (the St James's) 'Boys Brigade' as being 115 strong with the Parish turning out a procession of over 1300.

THE YOUNG LIFE PIONEERS & THE LIFE SAVING BRIGADE

The union of the B.L.B. and the B.B. in 1926 involved most of the companies in the two Brigades. Even without the 'model' rifles the B.B. Image in the 1920's remained very much centred around the older Boy; it was still visibly the descendant of the original 1st Glasgow Coy. modelled upon those part time soldiers; the 'Volunteers'. Many B.B. Coy's had been wearing khaki (until 1924) as part of their Cadet-Scheme affiliation.

Some B.L.B. Coy's however, were still fired with the pacifism of the early 1920's and regarded the Boys' Brigade as being simply too militaristic. They felt that it would be better to continue with the object of the B.L.B... 'To Save Life' and not to unite with the B.B. The national policy of the B.L.B., led by Donald Finnemore from Birmingham, was to unite so the dissidents had to 'go it alone'. Two typical examples are featured here'. The 'Young Life Pioneers' (London area) and The 'Life Saving Brigade' (W. Yorkshire). New companies of these Independent Life Brigades were formed in a decade when the popularity of organized uniformed youth groups reached its zenith and the epithet 'Life Saving' became particularly fashionable.

As the 1930's progressed, particularly after the great 1933 B.B. Jubilee Celebrations; perhaps as a result of the nation not wishing to look back to times of depression and conflict in society, fortunes for the 'Life Brigades' changed. Former dissidents and seperatists either re-joined the B.B., took up scouting or developed into non-uniformed Boys' Clubs.

1st Ilford Coy. Young Life Pioneers 1931

[R. Feasey]

The 1st Ilford Company were based at Ilford High Road Baptist Church. The above photo of the band, was taken in the 'Institute' Church Hall. Boys and Officers are resplendent in their full uniforms with 'service' pattern hats.

Young Life Pioneers Coy's. were formed in the London area, which had been a stronghold of the B.L.B. pre 1926. The 1st Ilford had been the 16th West Essex Coy. B.L.B. before giving up the title. Two of the most popular activities are pictured here; Camping & band. On the 'Band' picture the Capt is Mr Engle. Mr Rowland Brake was Bandmaster (That's him in the centre-front). Late on Parade and relegated to the back row was a young Officer Reg. Feasey who had joined the B.L.B. as a twelve year old.

By 1935 this Company, like other Y.L.P. Coys were asking to be re-admitted to the Boys' Brigade and they were accepted that year. Other Coys never re-joined but amalgamated with the 'Brotherhood of British Boy Scouts' an organisation with which they had been affiliated since B.L.B. days. (Those, presumably, with a large contingent of former B.L.B. Scouts).

In 1937 Reg Feasey took over as Captain of the B.B. Coy. now re-designated '16th Redbridge' where he remained as Capt for many years before being made Battalion President in 1972 and Hon. Life President in 1983. His son is now Coy. Capt. following in a family tradition.

1st Ilford Coy. Young Life Pioneers at Camp c1930

Note the Junior members uniforms.

[R. Feasey]

The Emblem of the Y.L.P.
Incorporating the Life belt, cross and crown of the B.L.B. with three chain links.

[Drawn up using available information]

1st Dewsbury Company. Life Saving Brigade. c1928

Based at Batley Carr Methodist Chapel, the company was formed about 1927 by three men from the church; William Edward Rayner, Fred Casson and Emile Pollard. Hearing about a 'Life Saving' Brigade' being formed in Leeds at the Whitehall Road Methodist Church, they went to meet its founder Colonel Blaxton. Suitably enthused with the idea of such a Brigade they returned to form the 1st Dewsbury Company L.S.B. Other Companies were formed nearby at Batley Carr Wesleyan and Commonside Methodist; all under the auspices of the 'Leeds Battalion' with the distinguished Col. Blaxton at the helm.

Ranks used by the L.S.B. were similar to the Boys' Life Brigade; Major and Warrant officer with the usual N.C.O.'s. Activities included a weekly drill parade, monthly church parade, band etc. Boys were allowed to join the L.S.B. when they would have only been old enough for the 'Life Boys' but not the B.B.... an important consideration, it seems, for the men who founded the Coy.

The photograph was taken outside their church (known locally as 'Upper Road Methodist Church' Batley Carr). Times were hard in the late 20's so uniforms are thin on the ground. Boys' full uniform consisted of; navy blue tunic with light blue piping on the collar, navy blue field service cap with light blue piping, company number and the letters 'L.S.B.', a 'white lanyard was also worn. (at least one Boy, Arthur Casson, is wearing a white haversack). Officers uniform included a navy blue tunic with collar badges and buttons, worn with a tie and white shirt, lanyard with whistle, service pattern hats with the L.S.B. Badge and ranks on the lower sleeve. Major Pollard is standing (left) and on the right is Fred Casson the Bandmaster wearing his blue 'band' sash. The three officers in the centre are (L to R) W/O. Joe Ineson, W/O Jimmy Ineson and Captain William E. Rayner. The emblem of the L.S.B. incorporated, as its centre the ubiquitous Life-Saving Red Cross. They were disbanded sometime in the early 1930's, perhaps because they never joined up with the Boys' Brigade.

Upper Road Methodist Church closed its doors in 1960 with the congregation going to other nearby churches. The impressive flight of steps like the chapel they lead to, have not been demolished or left to decay; former Chapel (& steps) live on as the 'Dewsbury Arts Centre'.

THE SPRING HOLIDAY.—(*Inspection of the Boys' Brigade, Glasgow Battalion.*)

A page from 'Quiz' Magazine   [*John Cooper*]

5. LITTLE BROTHER

As the 20th Century was young, so too was a large percentage of the British population. 'Boys' joining the Brigades were, in fact 'Youths' who had usually left school and were often holding down a regular job.

The streets were playgrounds for the younger brothers, with time on their hands; youngsters who ran along the road at the side of parades, trying to keep in step. Younger brothers who liked nothing more than dressing up and playing at 'soldiers'.

The Churches were lamenting the relatively small percentage of young attenders at their Sunday Schools, so perhaps it was inevitable that the Brigades would be asked to open their doors to the younger Boy; being careful, of course, to separate their activities from those of their seniors.

The last thing the Brigade Boy wanted whilst he was Drilling, doing Physical Exercises, Ambulance work or Band was to be surrounded by kids!

THE BOY RESERVES

1917-1926

Object: *'The advancement of Christ's Kingdom among young Boys and the training of a body of suitable recruits for The Boys' Brigade.*

The Boy Reserves came into being, like their 'big brothers' in the B.B. to meet an urgent need. An increasing number of B.B. Companies before 1917 were admitting Boys under the age of twelve years and giving them the name 'cadets'. The 3rd Oldham Coy. B.B. had a 'Junior B.B. Company' of thirty plus Boys complete with their own 'service' pattern hats… they were not alone. Sometimes these 'cadets' were being drilled with dummy rifles!

A decline in the number of younger Boys attending Sunday Schools soon brought suggestions for an organization which would make Sunday School attendance compulsory. Although the 1st World War was still raging, the matter was taken up with some urgency by the Boys' Brigade who asked Executive member F.C. Carey Longmore, Capt of 1st Warley (Essex) Coy, who had himself been experimenting with a pre-B.B. organization, to produce a workable scheme.

In Sept 1917 Carey Longmore's scheme was approved. The 1st Warley (Essex) at the Parish Church, was the first 'section' followed by 1st Beverley, 30th Liverpool, 14th Manchester & 1st Swansea. The name 'Boy Reserves' was suggested by Longmore who got the idea from the Regimental 'reserve' Battalions of untrained youths being taken on by the army at that time. Initially, drill took priority over games and no Lady leaders were allowed… the general view seemed to be that this was simply a stage towards becoming a B.B. Boy. One Officer wrote in the B.B. Gazette: *'It should be instilled into the nippers that they are merely caterpillars whose butterfly days are yet to come'* However, gradually games took priority and Lady Leaders were allowed.

Boys aged between 9 and 12 yrs were eligible to join. Uniform consisted of a 'sailor' pattern hat with 'Boy Reserves' in Blue on ribbon. Navy Blue jersey with crest sewn-on left-breast. Navy Blue Shorts. White Cap. covers and an optional navy blue shoulder pennant were added later. Also a metal badge was issued as an alternative to the cloth one. (The white lanyard indicated a 'Leading Boy'). The emblem was a B.B. Anchor with 'B.R.' instead of 'B.B.', enclosed by a shield border. In 1918 The Boy Reserves had 59 Sections with 1,573 Boys which by 1926 had increased to 646 sections with a total of 18,928 Boys.

[Reproduced with the kind permission of the Brigade Secretary of The Boys' Brigade]

13th Leeds Section Boy Reserves Session 1921/2
Note the cloth Jersey badges worn by this section.

68

Peckham Boy Reserves c1921
Note the brass badges worn by this Section. The Lady leaders are pictured wearing their 'Wren Officer' style hats ('Inflicted upon them' [His words] by Douglas Pearson Smith, Son of the B.B. Founder and co-founder of the original Boy Reserve Scheme with Carey Longmore… he was serving in the Royal Naval Air Service at the time.)

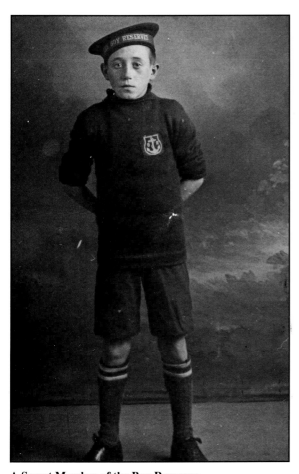

A Smart Member of the Boy Reserves
Note the Cloth Badge

'A rose between two thorns' Hilda Barnett and her Brigade brothers. 1918.

B.L.B. 'CADETS'

1st Dover Company B.L.B. c1909 with their 'cadets' (Front Row)
The young members (aged 10-12 yrs) are the 'Cadet' section of the Company, indicated by a 'C' in their forage caps. The 'Cadets' came into being in the B.L.B. around 1902 when the constitution mentions that 'Cadets' could form a special section of the Company with a uniform of cap, belt and haversack. It was emphasised that 'Cadets' should work quite separately from the rest of the Company, although they were allowed to precede the Company when on Parade.

The 'Cadets' continued until 1920 when the 'Lifeboys' was started as a replacement.

Note the stretcher prominently displayed at the front of the Company, reflecting the Brigade motto 'To Save Life'.

Worth Baptist Boys' Life Brigade (W. Sussex?)
The 'Cadets' here, don't have 'C's in their caps.

THE LIFEBOYS

The Junior League of The Boys' Life Brigade 1920-1926

In 1920 the B.L.B. decided that 'younger brother required a more completely organized plan' and The Lifeboys were formed.

The emblem was a Life Buoy enclosing four squares representing the four-sided programme; Educational, Social, Physical, and Devotional. Proficiency Badges were awarded on a group basis (each Lifeboy 'Team' was divided into 'groups'). 1st, 2nd & 3rd Class orders of merit could be earned by Boys and exchanged for a special Lifeboy transfer badge upon entering the B.L.B. Company.

The compulsory uniform consisted of: metal badge worn on a dark blue school cap. Saxe Blue jerseys with a woven badge and dark blue shorts were optional.

'On Parade'

The 'Lifeboy Code' was learnt by all Lifeboys: '*A member will be reverent, true, clean in speech and action; he will be loyal to his parents, his home, his Sunday School and his Team; he will do his best to follow his great leader, Jesus Christ; he will be a total abstainer.*'

In 1926 the Lifeboys had 322 teams and a total of 7,965 Boys.

[Reproduced with the kind permission of the Brigade Secretary of The Boys Brigade.]

Carlton Team. The Lifeboys. August 1925

Note: These Boys are wearing the full uniform. The words 'Life Boys' on the Lifebuoy should read as one word 'Lifeboys'

THE LIFE BOYS 1926-1966

Motto: 'Play the Game'

Object: *'The advancement of Christ's Kingdom among young Boys and the training of a body of suitable Recruits for The Boys' Brigade.'*

When on October 1st 1926 the Boys' Brigade and the Boys' Life Brigade united, so too did The Lifeboys and the Boy Reserves to form **The Life Boys.** Boys aged 9 yrs – 12 (later 8-12) could be members.

The Anchor emblem of the B.R. and the Lifebuoy of the Lifeboys were combined. Since the B.L.B. had sacrificed their name in becoming 'The Boys' Brigade' the 'Boy Reserves' changed to 'Life Boys' (Spelt in two words). Although the B.R. was numerically stronger, most of the 'Lifeboy' terminology was adopted by the new organization, in particular the 'four-square' principle. A 'seal' system was used for knowledge and skills in a wide variety of subjects.

Uniforms were amalgamated by a compromise. 'A' & 'B' uniforms were allowed Just as in the B.B. The 'A' being a naval pattern cap with 'The Life Boys' in blue (Later in gold) on ribbon; the badge with a crest either in metal or woven on ribbon was worn on the left breast. Blue Jersey and shorts could be worn. Blue pennants with metal numbers of the B.B. Coy. were worn on the right shoulder. 'Leading Boys' continued to wear lanyards (later white cap covers). The 'B' uniform was the school cap with metal badge on front, Saxe Blue Jersey with badge on let breast. Dark blue shorts, black stockings with two saxe blue stripes at the top. This 'B' uniform was discontinued in 1941 but the black stockings with two saxe blue stripes at the top were retained.

The Life Boys were composed of 'Teams' associated with B.B. Companies, under the Control of a 'Leader-In-Charge'.

By 1st Sept 1966 The Life Boys' 2,932 teams were 68,362 Boys strong. from that date however, they ceased to exist, becoming the 'Junior Section' of The Boys' brigade. Until 1970 the 'sailor hat' was still used with the words 'The Boys Brigade' on the ribbon. The Navy Blue Jerseys continued until 1971 with a woven B.B. Badge worn on the left breast.

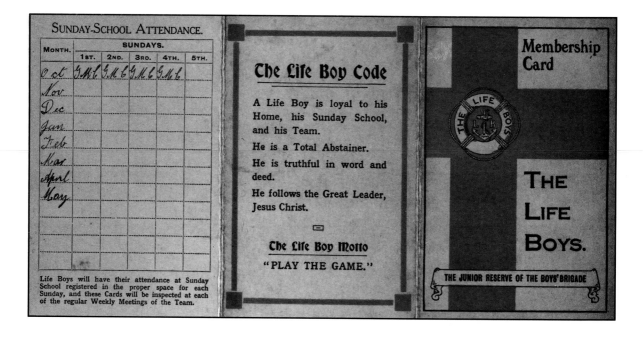

The 57th Birmingham Life Boy Team 1961
Associated with the 57th Birmingham Coy. B.B. Pheasey Methodist Church. Leaders L to R. Mr Jack Highfield, Mr Edgar Payne (Leader in charge) Mr John Plant, Mr Daniel Donohue ('Don'). The author is pictured amongst those Boys standing, third from left looking rather wistful. Memories of those late 1950's days in the Life Boys include rides in Don's brand new 'Utilabrake' often with virtually all of our team 'aboard' listening to his stories of life in the Navy. There was an intense group rivalry between the 'Lions', 'Leopards' and 'Tigers' only exceeded annually by malevolent and passionate team loyalty in our battle against the Cubs in the school playground when we proudly donned our uniforms for St. George's day. We polished our shoes on the back of our stockings just before inspection forgetting the dust on our Sailor-hats so skilfully skimmed, just minutes before, across the church car-park!

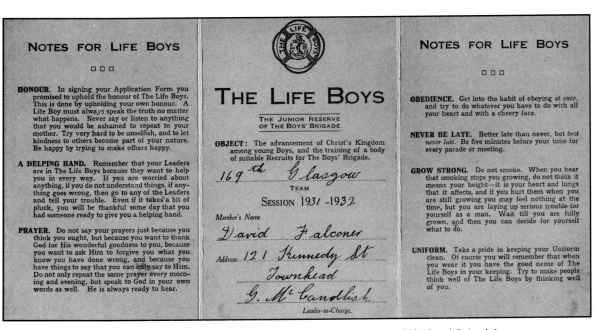

[Reproduced with the kind permission of the Brigade Secretary of The Boys' Brigade]

C.L.B. 'JUNIORS'

'Volunteers', C.L.B. Members & 'Juniors' c1900
During the South African Campaign the C.L.B. were encouraged to drill with the 'Volunteers'. As a consequence many Lads joined the Volunteers upon leaving the Brigade. A Volunteer Band is pictured here incorporating C.L.B. members. The young Boys at the front with model rifles are wearing a 'star' hat badge distinguishing them as 'Juniors'. The Official C.L.B. 'Training Corps' didn't start until 1913 so these lads were probably one of many 'unofficial' groups of Juniors associated with C.L.B. Coys.

Note the similarity between the uniforms of the 'Lads' of all ages.

Early C.L.B. Proforma

JUNIOR TRAINING CORPS
1913 –

YOUNG BOYS' CORPS
1936 –

The introduction of the Junior Training Corps and the Young Boys Corps for Junior members of the Church Lads' Brigade coincided with major changes in the C.L.B. in 1913 and 1936. Although the 1936 change was perhaps the more significant of the two, changes in uniform happened throughout the Brigade at both times.

THE JUNIOR TRAINING CORPS. For Boys aged 10-14 yrs, was started in 1913 just as the whole of the C.L.B. were adopting the Khaki Service Dress Uniform. 'Equipment' was worn over normal clothing; this consisted of a Webbing belt, haversack and cap. The Cap style changed from a 'Tam O' shanter' type to a more familiar field-service pattern although for a time both types were worn. By 1919 only the Field-Service type seems to have been in use with the J.T.C. metal badge on the side. In 1936 the 'Equipment' uniform was changed to a full uniform in keeping with the rest of the Brigade, retaining the cap, haversack and belt but including now a blue shirt, tie and ahorts and lanyard. The J.T.C. Corps medal could be worn on right breast over the pocket along with the ribbon brooch. The Proficiency Badge being worn over the other breast pocket. The J.T.C. had N.C.O.'s just like their big brothers, (Jnr L/Cpl, Jnr Cpl, not Sgt.), chevrons being worn on the right arm. Other badges and good conduct stripes were worn on the left arm.

THE YOUNG BOYS' CORPS. For Boys aged 8-10 yrs (Later 7-10 yrs) came into being during the 'Reformation' of the C.L.B. in 1935/6. In 1935 a new Blue Uniform had been adopted by all units which signified the Brigade's final parting with the 'Cadet' label. Cadet Affiliation and Recognition was abolished officially in 1936. The C.L.B. now had a new constitution and a new Corps for Young Boys.

The Y.B.C. had a uniform hat similar to the J.T.C. with Navy Blue Jersey bearing the initials 'Y.B.C.' on a cloth badge in the centre of the chest. A 'Proficiency Star' (Remarkably similar to those worn by the Juniors of 1900 on their forage caps), could be worn above the Y.B.C. Badge.

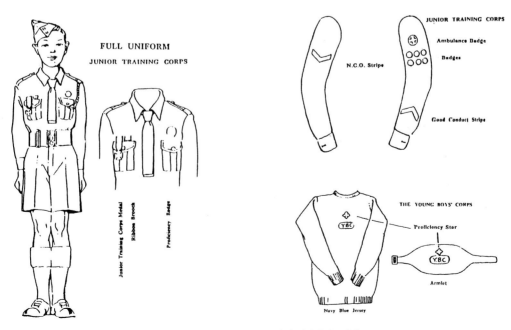

[The Church Lads' & Church Girls' Brigade]

75

A C.L.B. Co. from Manchester. c1913
J.T.C. members are wearing 'Pill Box' hats with J.T.C. Badges and standard C.L.B. Belts.

Halifax C.L.B. with their J.T.C. members c1913
Note the 'Tam o'shanter' hats

J.T.C. Boys at a May Day Pageant 1919
Note the two C.L.B. Lads in Khaki who seem to have been left in charge of the Boys.

A London Diocesan C.L.B. Junior c1920
Note the leather waistbelt and neckerchief. Jerseys or shirts were worn

Edgar, in his London Diocesan C.L.B. (Junior) uniform. c1920.

Three Smart Juniors And their Sister... c1919. Note the Field-Service Caps & Wide Webbing belts

Two brothers from Hull. c1914
The younger brother, on the right, is in the J.T.C.

HOME...
A Smart C.L.B. Company c1937
Note: They are wearing their new Blue Uniform. All three sections are represented, including the J.T.C. in their new full uniforms and the Y.B.C. Many Brigade companies grew large on the massive inter-war housing estates.

AND AWAY ...
J.T.C. Boys from Holy Trinity Church, Rotherhithe at the Long Ditton Camp. 1930s.
Most Brigades had their own 'Junior' organizations. The Boys' Own Brigade started a 'Junior Corps' in Liverpool in 1913 for Boys under 12 yrs, but over 10 yrs.

[Ronnie Halliwell]

No 8 Co. Bolton B.B. 1939. Officers, Instructors, Cadets & 'Bantam Boys'
This picture was taken outside their H.Q. in Park St. Bolton. The three young lads are members of the B.B.B.'s own Junior Reserve the 'Bantam Boys' who had a uniform cap with an inverted 'V' stripe pattern and Co. Number. The striped ties were also uniform; the wearing of a Jersey was optional.

[The Boys Brigade. Glasgow Battalion]

All Good Things Come to an End......Discharge Certificate 1905
A Boys' time in the Brigade was something special, a time to be remembered for the rest of his life, memories to be treasured, friendships recalled. The end of membership was officially marked by the presentation of a 'discharge certificate'. This example of 1905 portrays the various activities as a reminder of past involvement.

The Brigades gave to Boys, and still give, much that is not tangible like a certificate but of greater value: A pattern and purpose to their lives.

BIBLIOGRAPHY

Anderson, J.F. *21 Years History 1st Aberdeen Coy. Boys' Brigade. Aberdeen, Thomson & Duncan 1907.*

Barnard, H.C. *A History of English Education from 1760. London. Univ. of London. 1947.*

Birch, A. *The Story of the Boys' Brigade. London, Frederick Muller, 1959.*

Boys Brigade Omnibus, The, London & Glasgow, Collins 1957.

Boys' Brigade, The, Archive Press Series. Eleven Titles, London, 1984.

Boys' Brigade, The, Camp Handbook, Glasgow B.B. Headquarters. 1909.

Boys' Brigade, The, Birmingham Battalion, Camp orders & Regulations. 1914.

Boys' Brigade, The, Jubilee Book. Boys' Brigade London & Glasgow. 1933.

Boys' Brigade, The, B.B. Gazette. 1890's – 1990.

Boys' Brigade, The, 'The B.B.' an illustrated monthly for Boys. Vol. I 1895. Vol III 1897

Boys' Brigade, The, Souvenir of 13th Cardiff Coy. Camp Southampton Aug. 1908. [Unpublished presentation book]

Boys' Brigade, The, Ambulance Handbook – B.B. Headquarters, London & Glasgow. 1952.

Boys' Own Brigade, The, Report of Executive Committee, 1st Annual Council Meeting, 1909.

Brew, J.M. *In the Service of Youth, A Practical Manual of work among adolescents, London, Faber & Faber 1943.*

Bolsover Colliery Co. The, Jubilee Book. 1889-1939. Nottingham. 1939.

Butcher, J.W. *Beware of Imitations, Talks to Boys. London Our Boys & Girls Office. c1910.*

Butcher, J.W. *Boys' Brigade & Other Talks, London Charles H Kelly c1909*

Carpenter P. (Ed) *Challenge. The Duke of Edinburgh's Award in Action. London. Ward Lock 1966.*

Catholic Boys' Brigade, The, C.B.B. Gazette. 1910, 1911 1913 etc.

Catholic Boys' Brigade, The, C.B.B. Annual Report. 1908, 1910, 1913 etc.

Catholic Boys' Brigade, The, Catalogue of Musical Instruments, c1905.

Catholic Boys' Brigade, The, List of Uniform, Equipment and Drill Books.

Catholic Boys' Brigade, The, Plum Duff Magazine. No 1. G. Pauling (Ed) 1905.

Catholic Boys' Brigade, The, Price List of Equipment & Accessories. Uniform Clothing & Equipment Co.

Catholic Boys' Brigade, The, St. Ignatius Stamford Hill Co. 2nd Annual Report. April 1906.

Christian Life Magazine, Unitarian. Bound Volume. 1913

Church Lads' Brigade, The, 1907 Camp Appeal Booklet.

Church Lads' Brigade, The, Brigade Magazine, Bound Volumes. 1913-1965.

Church Lads' Brigade, The, Pocket Book, Regulations etc. 1931.

Church Lads' Brigade, The, Camp Arrangements, Midland District Camp, Rhyl 1911.

Collis, H. with Hurll F. and Hazlewood R. *B.P.'s Scouts: An Official History of the Boy Scouts association. London: Collins, 1961.*

Davies, J. *The Victorian Kitchen. London. B.B.C. Books. 1989.*

Dawes, F. *A Cry From the Streets. The Boys' Club Movement 1850's to Present. London. Wayland 1975.*

Drummond H. *First! A Talk with the Boys' Brigade, The B.B. H.Q. Office, Glasgow. 1889.*

Eagar, W. McG. *Making Men: The History of Boys' Clubs and Related Movements in Gt. Britain. London: University of London Press, 1953.*

Evans, E.J. Richards J. *A Social History of Britain In Postcards 1870-1930. London Longman. 1980.*

Farquharson J. & Sons. List of Boys' Brigade Accoutrements & Accessories. c1909.

Gibbon, F.P. *Comrades under Canvas: London. R.T.S. c1908.*

Gibbon F.P. *William A Smith of the Boys' Brigade. London: Collins, 1934.*

Henriques, B.L.G. *Club Leadership. London Humphrey Milford. O.U.P. 1933.*

Horn P. Sutton P.A. *The Victorian & Edwardian Schoolchild. Gloucester. Alan Sutton. 1989.*

Humphries S, Mack J, Perks R, *A Century of Childhood. London, Sidgwick & Jackson. 1988.*

Hutton Sir. E. Lt. Gen. *A Brief History of the King's Royal Rifle Corps 1755-1915. (2nd Ed) Winchester. Warren & Sons. 1917.*

Inquirer Magazine, Unitarian. Bound Volumes 1900-1925.

Jenkinson E.J. Et Al. *Boys of the Brigade & Other stories of Adventure & School Life. London Epworth 1933.*

Lund, B & M *Edwardian Childhood on Old Picture Postcards, Nottingham. Reflections. 1988.*

Liverpool Domestic Miss. Soc. 2 Log Books 'Boys' Own Brigade' 1910/15. No 7 Coy. Liverpool Record Office. 266 DOM./16/1-2.

Magnus C.L. *'E.M.J.' The Man & His Work. Ernest Joseph. London. Private Pub. 1962.*

McFarlan, D. *First For Boys, The Story of The Boys' Brigade 1883-1983. Glasgow, Collins 1982*

Morning Light Magazine. New Church. Bound Volumes 1896-1914.

Moyes, L. *The Boys Brigade in Bolton, 100 years of Service for Youth 1887-1987. Bolton B.B. 1987.*

Oakton. G. *Tape Recorded Interview. Birmingham. January 1990.*

Onlooker Magazine. The Stedfast Association London Newsletter. 1983-1990.

Orphan Homes of Scotland School, Bridge of Weir. Reports. 1911-1918, 1933, 1936-37, 1940, 1943, 47, 48

Pain, G.S. *Boys' Clubs. A Practical Handbook. London. Ludgate Circus House. 1928.*

Peacock, Roger S. *Pioneer of Boyhood: The Story of Sir William A Smith, founder of The Boys' Brigade. Glasgow: The Boys' Brigade, 1954.*

Pierce A.J. & D.K. *Victorian and Edwardian Children From Old Photographs. London. B.T. Batsford. 1980.*

Reed, B.H. *Eighty Thousand Adolescents, Young People in Birmingham. London. George Allen & Unwin. 1950.*

Reid, H. *Knights of the Anchor, & other talks. Church of Scotland Youth Committee. Edinburgh. 1938.*

Reid, H. *The Luck of The Stedfast. Adventures of three B.B. Comrades. London & Glasgow, Collins (2nd Ed.) 1933.*

Reid, H. *Private James Fyffe. A Story of The Boys' Brigade. London & Glasgow. Collins (2nd Ed) 1935.*

Reid, H. *Play the Man. Talks with Boys on the Battle of Life. Edinburgh, Oliphant, Anderson & Ferrier, 1900.*

Rosenthal M. *The Character Factory, London. Collins 1986.*

Russell C.E.B. & L. *Lads' Clubs, Their History, Organization & Management, London. A & C Black. 1932.*

Stedfast Mag. E.R. Staniford (Ed). Oct 1953-1979.

Smith, J. *Edwardian Children, London, Hutchinson 1983.*

Springhall, J.O. *Youth, Empire & Society: British Youth Movements, 1883-1940. London Croom Helm, 1977.*

Springhall, J.O. Fraser, B. and Hoare M. *Sure & Stedfast: A History of the Boys' Brigade, 1883-1983. London; Collins, 1983.*

Wakeling A.L. *Brightlingsea Society of the New Church. A History 1813-1968. Priv. Pub. 1968.*

Walker G.H. *W.A. Smith, A Man Who Had Something To Say. London. The B.B. London District. 1971.*

Wade, E.K. *The Story of Scouting. London: C. Arthur Pearson, 1935.*

Westlake R.A. *A Register of Territorial Force Cadet Units 1910-1922. Pub. Private. 1984.*

Williams R. *Essex Church In Kensington. 1887-1987. History of a Unitarian Cause. Private Pub. 1987.*

Young People's Magazine. The New Church. Bound Volumes. 1901-1904.

Young England Magazine. Bound Volumes. 1912-1918.

[John Cooper]

FURTHER INFORMATION about the organisations featured in this book may be obtained from:

THE BOYS' BRIGADE

King's Terrace,
1, Galena Road,
Hammersmith,
LONDON W6 0LT

Tel: 081 741 4001

THE CHURCH LADS' AND CHURCH GIRLS' BRIGADE

2, Barnsley Road,
Wath Upon Dearne,
Rotherham,
SOUTH YORKSHIRE S63 6PY

Tel: 0709 876535

JEWISH LADS' AND GIRLS' BRIGADE

Camperdown House,
3, Beechwood Road,
South Woodford,
LONDON E18 1LA

Tel: 081 989 8990

THE SCOUT ASSOCIATION

Baden-Powell House,
Queen's Gate,
LONDON SW7 5JS

Tel: 071 584 7030

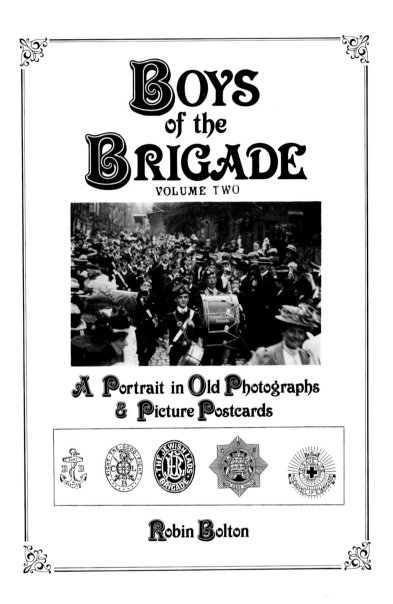

BOYS of the BRIGADE
VOLUME TWO

A Portrait in Old Photographs & Picture Postcards

Robin Bolton

The Contents include:
War Service, Summer Camp,
Scouting, Bands, Street Parades,
Ambulance, Sports. Etc.